MW00950511

Bipolar Disorder: My Biggest Competitor
An Olympian's Journey with Mental Illness

A Memoir by Amy Gamble

© 2017 by Amy Gamble. All rights reserved.

No part of this book may be reproduced in any written, electronic, recording, or photocopying without written permission of the publisher or author. The exception would be in the case of brief quotations embodied in the critical articles or reviews and pages where permission is specifically granted by the publisher or author.

Although every precaution has been taken to verify the accuracy of the information contained herein, the author and publisher assume no responsibility for any errors or omissions. No liability is assumed for damages that may result from the use of information contained within.

This book is dedicated to my mom, who has always inspired me,
and to the many people who are impacted by mental illness.

Acknowledgements

There are many people who have helped me in my life journey. Here are a few who are very special to me.

First and foremost is my mother, who is the eternal optimist. Never once did she waver in her support of my dreams. Also, my sister Shelley, who has been one of my biggest cheerleaders, and my sisters Cindy and Sherry, who helped me become a successful athlete. My nieces, Natalie and Ashley, and my nephew Issac—who have supported me with unconditional love.

Thanks to my cousin Christy, who has always been there for me.

My gratitude to my family at the National Alliance on Mental Illness (NAMI) Greater Wheeling, WV who helped me take the next step in my recovery journey, and especially to my friend Libby, who is one of the most beautiful people I have ever met.

The folks at the Marian House, who always brightened my spirits with their greetings and smiles, have been shining examples of what is really important in life.

My church family at The Experience Church and Pastors Tim and Linda Seidler for supporting me right where I am.

Dr. Maura Andronic is the most amazing psychiatrist. She helped me back to a life worth living.

My editor Lori Whitwam, who helped shape the book into something I could be proud of.

And to all my social media friends on Facebook, WordPress, and Twitter. I am grateful for all your encouraging comments.

Foreword

I met Amy after she recovered from her last psychotic episode. She was already stable on medications, and we only had to make some adjustments to deal with the sedative side effects.

After this, Amy's recovery really took off.

But she still had to take one important step: to come to terms with the illness and acquire effective coping skills to deal with it.

This brave book is exactly the result of this difficult process and shows how wonderfully she mastered this task.

Bipolar Disorder: My Biggest Competitor is the heart-wrenching story of an Olympian's struggle with and eventual triumph over the terrifying highs and lows of the bipolar disorder.

Through scenes of astonishing visceral and emotional power, Amy takes us from the successful team handball Olympian at the 1988 Seoul Games to the darker side of bipolar disorder.

This is a strong, thorough biographical writing, woven from multiple perspectives which, through the vivid and real-life examples, provides a glimpse into her struggles with bipolar disorder.

With remarkable honesty and humor, Amy shows the effects of this illness on the mind, body, and soul of those who suffer with it. And also, at the same time, she strives to separate the diagnosis from the individual living with it.

However, despite the struggles, this is not a book that brings the reader down, rather a road map for wellness and a vastly informative yet entertaining guided tour of bipolar disorder for those who don't understand it.

I particularly appreciate the insights into her deeply personal and intense experiences, which help others understand this cruel illness. This is why individual stories like this are crucial in dissolving stereotypes, shifting public perception of mental illness, and combating stigma.

This memoir is an excellent guide to a painful and difficult yet treatable illness. Amy's courage in sharing her experience is impressive and commendable. It will help others struggling with this illness feel less isolated and more hopeful.

Maura Andronic, MD
Psychiatrist

Introduction

Most people do not understand mental illness because, as a culture, we haven't done a very good job of talking about it. Mental illness is entrenched in people's psyches like a bad horror movie that gives you nightmares. But the great news is more and more celebrities are stepping up and discussing their struggles. This helps people realize they are not alone, and it takes a dent out of the shame attached to mental illness. Several advocacy groups are increasing their efforts to educate, create awareness, and eliminate the stigma. The noise is getting louder, the message clearer. Millions of people live with mental illness.

I live with bipolar disorder, and I have family members who live with it as well, but I am also an Olympian, a former college basketball player, a person who has worked in corporate America for many years, a daughter, a sister, a friend, an inspirational speaker, and a fierce mental health advocate. I am not crazy, wacko, loony, nuts, dangerous, psycho, or violent. When I teach Mental Health First Aid, almost every class will fill up the flip chart page with negative words they've heard about people with mental illness. But I am here to tell you those words are disparaging and come from those who are filled with fear of the unknown.

I want to help you understand what it is like to live with a severe mental illness. And I want you to know what it's like to watch your loved ones become affected by it, because mental illness is a family disease. I have the perspective of being in the seat of someone who lives with mental illness and being a loved one who has watched family members struggle. My drive for mental health advocacy comes from those perspectives.

Despite having been on a world stage competing against great opponents, I have found no greater competitor than bipolar disorder. In fact, I believe any person who lives with a mental disorder has great strength and resilience. These are the qualities necessary to live with and beat mental illness.

It will take me a lifetime to control my bipolar disorder, but each day I get out of bed and do something productive I mark down as a win. There is no cure for bipolar disorder, but there are medications that help me live a relatively normal life. I am able to work, contribute to my community, and have meaningful relationships. No matter what has happened to me, I refuse to let bipolar disorder keep me from my dreams. I battle this illness every day. Some days I lose, some days I win.

This is my story.

Facing the Truth

The blinders have been removed
She has taken her gloves off and removed her coat
She sits in stillness with peaceful knowing
Knowing from the soul
Inspired by the spirit
The storm came along with no warning
It whirled and twirled devastation
Leaving people shocked, hurt, stunned and dismayed
The creation of fear perpetuated
Numbness permeated and opened wounds
Left behind were the remnants of missing pieces
The young woman an old soul stood strong
But the powerful force of the storm threw her to
unconsciousness
When she awoke it was apparent to her she was the storm
Crushed by the aftermath of viewing what she left behind
Deeply saddened with what she unknowingly had done
Egotistically embarrassed, ashamed and guilty
Incapable of seeing what the mirrors were telling her
Her prayers were answered one day
She ask to be shown so she could heal
She prayed for strength and courage
She prayed for forgiveness of self and others
She lay helpless crying for hours in her bed
She faced her naked body and viewed her own destruction
Overtaken by grief, hurt, sadness, disappointment
But inspired by unconditional love
She is a person hurt by her past
She is a human being
She is not defined by labels
She is not willing to give up
She is walking her journey one step at a time
Who is she?
Who is this woman with such great strength?
She is not alone

— Amy Gamble

There is no greater agony than bearing an untold story inside you.

— Maya Angelou

Chapter 1

How Did This Happen?

In January 2013, I was sitting on the edge of my bunk in a jail cell. I was in a small town off Interstate 90 in the beautiful big sky country of Montana, where tall mountains rose above the horizon in a picturesque view.

A corrections officer had given me a few magazines to read. I casually shuffled through, stopping when I saw a person who had been to my home several times on the cover of *Ladies Home Journal*. I was so happy to read her story of healthiness and success, yet I felt a shocking sense of reality pierce through my bones. Life had taken me down some long, dark pathways, and in the moment, sitting in a tiny jail cell, all I could think of was how I could have let this happen to me. I was a long way from socializing with a celebrity.

I sat on a plastic covered foam mattress with a thin wool blanket to keep me warm, in a small cellblock with two separate cells and four bunks. At night, I felt claustrophobic because the door to my cell was locked, meaning I could not pace the floor other than three steps from my bunk, a far cry from the five-bedroom home I had been fortunate to live in. The cell had a stainless steel sink and toilet, and a holder to hang the rough, white, standard-issue towel. A Martha Stewart soft towel, it was not.

It was like I was watching a movie with two different characters—the Olympian and All-American small-town girl, versus the mentally ill, unemployed inmate. How did I resolve such tension between two characters that I knew were one and the same?

My situation finally sank into my mind in a sobering way. I had become another statistic in the column of people with bipolar disorder who had been in trouble with the legal system. And what made matters worse was this was not my first time.

It didn't matter that I had been under the treatment of a psychiatrist. No one seemed to care that I had been released from a hospital long before I was stable. All that mattered now was figuring out how I was going to get out of the mess. In my heart, I knew there would be a time when I could tell my story and people would understand it was not my fault.

I had questions for everyone. God, the people closest to me, my family, the mental health treatment system—and, most importantly, myself. Why did no one explain serious mental health issues to me? Why did it take my ninth hospitalization before someone educated me about bipolar disorder and how to manage it? Why did I not know or understand the impact of the stigma? Why did hospitals never keep me admitted long enough to stabilize my illness, always putting my well-being at risk? Why didn't I manage my illness better? Why couldn't I get the proper care?

Why me?

I was someone who worked in the healthcare industry. I understood the whole idea of early intervention strategies improving patient outcomes. In other words, get treatment after the first episode, stay with it, and do better than people who do not get treatment. I finally realized if these things could happen to someone like me, they could happen to anyone.

I had access to healthcare and good insurance. But stigma, denial, and a serious lack of understanding about how destructive bipolar disorder could be if not adequately treated influenced my path. It is the nature of the disease and the unintended impact of not managing a mental illness properly, and dealing with the taboo of mental illness that is entrenched in our history. The mentally ill have never had an easy path. Suffering is guaranteed, but how much suffering depends on each individual situation. I needed to hear the raw, harsh reality of how living with a severe, untreated, chronic mental illness could have a disastrous outcome. I was now another example of how that could happen.

It finally hit me. I had a serious mental illness, and I needed to learn how to live with it. While I passed the time playing blackjack with a deck of cards, sitting on my bunk bed in the jail cell, I contemplated what I was going to do to take back my life. In my mind, I asked myself to choose, and the conversation went something like this.

"Wow! What a mess I've gotten into. I really wish I was on the basketball court coaching my sixth-grade boys' team. That's where I was last year at this time. What a difference a year makes. What am I going to do about it? What if I go to prison? Oh my God, why did this have to happen to me?"

I had to overcome an extraordinary amount of adversity to reach the point where I took something so incredibly devastating and used all that negative energy in a positive way. One of the biggest lessons I learned was how much my guilt made me suffer. For me, it was less painful to spend three weeks in jail than it was to endure the torture from my own mind, not from the mental illness, but from the repetitive negative self-talk that destroyed what little sense of self I had left.

I'm one of the lucky ones who did not end up with a lengthy prison sentence. I was spared by the justice system that took mercy on me because they knew I was not a criminal, but a person affected by mental illness. And the fact that a treatment facility released me long before I was stable helped prove my case that I was a victim as well. Many people are not as fortunate as I was. This is why the top three mental health treatment facilities in the United States are the Cook County Jail in Chicago, the Los Angeles County Jail, and the Dade County Jail in Miami.

By sharing my story, I hope to make an impact on people's lives. I want those who need treatment to not be afraid to get help, and to understand that the consequences of untreated bipolar disorder can be quite severe. I want to add fuel to the fire of mental health advocates who know very well that the mental health treatment system is far beyond broken. Too many lives are lost or discarded because society cannot figure out how to provide the necessary number of hospital beds. Often, people can't get the proper inpatient care they need. Usually, the hospital stay is not determined by the course of their illness; rather it is based on how many days an insurance company will pay. And in most cases, the fact there is a shortage of inpatient psychiatric hospital beds means a person who is "better off" may be released early so a person who is "worse off" can have the bed.

It has been a long journey learning how to manage bipolar disorder. I'm just sorry it took me so long to understand my biggest competitor as it tried to steal my life out from under me. I felt like a boxer who had stepped into the ring with a rugged, bullying opponent who didn't play fair. I took my hits. My face was bloody, my eyes blackened, my nose broken, and my pride destroyed. But each time I got knocked down, I got back up again. I refused to relinquish the title of my life to a mental illness. It's easy to look back and think about all the things that might have changed my outcome at any time. But I don't want to live my life in the past or with regret. I decided if I was going to beat bipolar disorder, I was going to have the last say.

Bipolar disorder may have almost knocked me out, but in the end, I'm happy to say I am now winning.

Chapter 2

Trouble at Home

I don't love anything about bipolar disorder. Bipolar disorder causes unusual mood swings and shifts in a person's energy levels. It was previously known as manic-depressive illness. Some people say they like the mania because it gives them lots of creative energy. And I've heard people say they don't mind the depression; in those dark moments, they do some of their best writing. Personally, I don't find anything pleasing about it, but perhaps it's because I have lived a lifetime with the negative impacts of bipolar disorder.

In 1984, I had just finished my freshman year playing women's college basketball at the University of Tennessee for legendary coach Pat Summitt. My team had made it to the NCAA National Championship title game, but fell short of victory in the finals, losing to the University of Southern California. I had been a highly recruited player and a high school All-American, which meant I had a lot of choices of colleges to attend. I chose the University of Tennessee because I wanted to play for Pat Summitt. But in my freshman year, I failed to meet the expectations of my coaches and myself. I had kept a secret from everyone that I was losing my number one supporter, my mom, to the struggles of mental illness.

It started when my mom and I were driving home from my recruiting visit to Tennessee. Mom literally cried all five hundred miles of the trip home.

I looked at my father, who was driving, and said, "What is wrong with her?"

"I don't know." He rolled his eyes, marking the end of our discussion of my mother's moods.

From that point on, she became a little more depressed every day. When I called her from college, sometimes she seemed so distant, like she was completely detached. I felt utterly alone in the world, holding on to a secret I couldn't share with anyone. My mom was in the throes of a depressive episode, and there was nothing I could do. My duel with bipolar disorder had begun. And for many years, I would be on the wrong end of the sword.

* * *

Several months passed, and I was nearing the end of school. Mom had gone to Baltimore, Maryland to visit one of my three sisters. While there, she was picked up by a police officer as she was walking down the street outside of Baltimore and taken to the emergency room. She was wearing a bathing suit and displaying erratic behavior. Thankfully, the officer noticed something was off and took her to the hospital instead of the police station. The problem, though, arose with the emergency room providers who prescribed my mom an antidepressant and sent her on her way. This was my first real experience with what I would later learn was a manic episode, and the beginning of a very long chapter in the book of life with mental illness.

I will never forget the day I arrived home from college at the end of my freshman year. I was unpacking for the summer when I received a call from my Uncle Fred telling me Mom had an accident and was in the hospital. My basketball teammate Mary O. and her sister Beth lived in Parkersburg, West Virginia, and she often gave me a ride from Knoxville to her hometown. Someone in my family would pick me up and drive me the two hours north to Glen Dale. I don't recall who had given me a ride that summer, but I do know it wasn't my mother.

When the call came from Uncle Fred, I was sitting on the floor in my bedroom unpacking a gigantic, oversized suitcase that had nearly all the clothes I owned. I answered the phone, rather annoyed and irritable because I'd had little sleep the night before.

In his gentle voice, he said, "Amy, your mom's been in a bad accident."

"What happened?" I was confused.

"She's fallen off a balcony, and she's hurt real bad. But she'll be okay."

After those words, everything else became a blur. More phone calls. More confusing explanations. My stress level was off the charts. Later, I found out this terrible accident was related to a mental health crisis, and she was very fortunate to be alive. Emotionally, it was like a volcano had erupted inside my heart and left me raw with inexplicable debris. Stress had pushed my anxiety to a new high, and I dealt with it by numbing my emotions. It was the only way I knew how to cope. I just sat on the floor unable to do anything, especially not cry.

The incident occurred five hours away from our home in West Virginia. My mother had been very upset with my father, and in her state of mind she wanted nothing to do with him. As a family, we all decided it was best he not go to the hospital. The first thing I did after receiving the news was call my other sisters, Sherry, Shelley, and Cindy.

Cindy was living in North Carolina and had not yet decided if she would make the trip. Shelley had been recovering from her own health problems. And Sherry had been the last one to see our mother, so she was in the position to answer the questions the rest of us had. She was already in Baltimore, pleading with someone to come and help her. I was the only one able to help, and I was just nineteen years old.

I remember my dad saying, "I'll go with you. You don't need to go by yourself."

I looked into my father's sad, blue eyes. "She doesn't want you there. It's best you stay home." I walked past him and threw my duffle bag in the car.

A couple hours after receiving the dreadful phone call, I put on my best Tennessee gear and got behind the wheel of my mom's blue Monte Carlo and set out for Baltimore.

Amy Gamble

Wearing my Lady Vol gear made me confident and comforted me. I was "somebody" because I played for Tennessee and Pat Summitt, and that was a surge of confidence I needed in that moment.

I had no map, personal GPS was not yet available, and I truly did not know where I was going. It's hard to believe, but I did what I always do when I'm lost, scared, or need encouragement—I prayed. And somehow, I found my way right to the hospital entrance.

When I arrived at the hospital, I was met by an emotionally distressed doctor.

"I'm here to see Esther Gamble," I said to the nurse behind the desk.

The doctor jumped up from his seat. "Are you the daughter?" Before I could answer, he rapidly continued. "Your mother had a psychotic episode. She has manic-depressive illness or schizophrenia. You need to convince your mother she should sign herself in voluntarily, or I'm going to send her to the state institution. You don't want that to happen to her, do you?"

"No, I don't," I said sheepishly.

"Talk to her, then. Okay?"

I had no idea what those words meant. The only thing I was certain of was that I didn't want Mom to end up in the state psychiatric hospital. It didn't sound like a good place. My mind went directly to imagining the old insane asylums, which had horrible reputations for abuse and neglect. My job was to talk her into voluntarily signing herself in for psychiatric treatment. If she refused to sign, the doctor threatened to involuntarily commit her to the state hospital.

There wasn't internet as we now know it back in 1984, so I took myself to the library to look up the words the doctor had thrown at me. At nineteen years old, I learned the meaning of involuntary commitment, manic-depressive illness, schizophrenia, psychosis, delusions, and hallucinations—words that are still not well understood by the general public.

Every now and then, I come across the yellow legal pad with all those words written in black ink. For some reason, I have held onto that piece of paper after all these years. I suspect it is my way of acknowledging the monumental impact the event had on my life, and my cerebral way of dealing with it. I have learned my logical side has helped me through more than one patch of tough times.

During that time, I was terrified. My only frame of reference for mental illness were the sensational stories about my Great Aunt Yetti, who spent most of her life in a psychiatric hospital with a diagnosis of manic-depressive illness, and my great-grandfather, Samuel, who died by suicide, having endured a lifelong battle with what my mother said was severe depression. Yetti and Samuel were not related, but they were both from my mother's side of the family.

But back then, people didn't talk about mental illness. My grandfather was only in fifth grade and had to drop out of school following his father's suicide to take care of his six brothers and sisters. He was thirteen years old.

I remember hearing the story about how Aunt Yetti was let out of the hospital for a little while, only to be put back in for the rest of her life after tossing her husband's clothes in a huge pile in the front yard and setting them on fire. I never really understood all the details about Aunt Yetti. I only knew I felt sorry for her. She ended up dying from cancer in that state institution, which has since been torn down.

I was beyond afraid; I was numb with fear for Mom. I didn't want to see her locked away in a psychiatric hospital, yet she'd had a psychotic episode and run from someone she thought was the devil. This person had scared her so much that she jumped off a thirty-foot balcony.

In her words, "It was a miracle I survived. God knew my business on Earth was not finished yet."

Mom was fortunate she survived. She ended up with fractured vertebrae, three cracked ribs, and a dislocated elbow. Miraculously, she landed on the small strip of grass bordering the sidewalk, and it probably saved her life.

When I walked into her hospital room, I had no idea what to expect. She looked pretty "normal" to me. I walked in and said, "How are you feeling?"

"I'm fine," she stated matter-of-factly.

I really didn't know what to think, until she continued talking and her thoughts seemed a little out of sorts—a mixture of reality and the leftover effects of psychosis.

"Mom, the doctors tell me you need to sign yourself in for psychiatric care."

"I'm not signing anything. I don't need *help*!" she replied, very irritated with me.

"Please, sign the papers. If you don't, they'll send you to the state psychiatric hospital. You don't want that, do you?"

She was silent for what seemed like an eternity. Then she finally said, "All right, I'll sign the damn papers."

I hurried out to the nurses' station and told the doctor, "She says she'll sign your papers."

The staff rushed into the room and put documents in front of her on a clipboard. She signed then tossed the pen back at them and gave me a very dirty look.

I left when they came and transported her to the psych unit in the "good" hospital. I drove over to Sherry's apartment where the accident had happened. Sherry was deeply upset and had been notified by the landlord that because of the incident she was going to be evicted.

I was at Sherry's apartment for no longer than an hour before we began to argue.

"How did you let this happen?" I demanded, raising my voice.

"It's not my fault. She's crazy. And she can't stay with me anymore," she said, raising her voice over mine.

"She's not crazy. She's sick, and she'll get better."

The argument continued in a circular way until I started to cry.

"I'm not staying here with you." My voice quivered with emotion, but I was trying to be tough. I picked up my small duffle bag and headed out the door. I got in the car and set off to find a hotel nearby.

Shortly after I got settled in the hotel, I went to the airport in Baltimore and picked up my sister, Cindy. She had flown in from North Carolina to help out. Not that Cindy could make the situation go away, but having someone else there was a huge support. I didn't feel all alone. Cindy was also a nurse, so she knew some of the psychiatric lingo. It was a relief to have her there.

We only stayed in the hotel a couple of days. Cindy and I visited Mom in the psych ward. The only thing I remember about it was being really bright white. Not a lot of decorations on the walls—just very sterile, as if it were a laboratory.

They told us at the hospital that Mom was trying to take her own life.

I insisted, "She told me it was an accident, and I believe her."

They looked at me like I was some naïve kid who had no idea what was really going on. But I knew mother better than anyone. If she said she wasn't trying to kill herself, that was the truth.

Mom only spent three weeks in the hospital in Baltimore then returned home to West Virginia. I spent the summer with her and my father. To keep Mom's mind occupied, I'd come up with activities for her like putting old pictures in albums. It was a good way to help ground her in reality and reflect on positive memories.

As a women's college basketball player, I also spent much of my summer working out and preparing for the next season. The stress of dealing with Mom gave me a boost of energy, and it helped me train for more than eight hours a day. I also worked as a camp counselor at three different basketball camps in West Virginia; Chapel Hill, North Carolina; and Towson, Maryland.

After I spent a week working at basketball camp at a small college not too far from my home, I returned home one evening. I had talked to no one while I was gone, so I was stunned to find my mother sleeping in my bed. Her eyes were wide eyed and dilated when I turned on the light.

My mind began to race with thoughts. "What do I do? What do I say? Is she crazy?" If I said I wasn't scared, that would be a lie. I put my things down and made my bed on the couch in the living room where I would sleep for the next two months. Anytime I heard a noise in the back bedroom, I would wake, and the surge of anxiety would pierce through my body.

During that summer, I told my coaches and the people closest to me what had happened with Mom. I'm not sure anyone knew how to handle the situation. Many people were very kind and compassionate, and others were cold and distant. At that time, no one discussed mental health issues, certainly not psychosis or the tragic situations that sometimes occur from untreated, severe mental illness.

One kind gesture was when one of the assistant coaches from Tennessee brought me a pair of basketball shoes at a camp I was working in Towson, Maryland. It wasn't the Adidas high top basketball shoes with the orange stripe that I appreciated most. It was Coach Nancy listening to my story. She was kind and compassionate. I remember the exchange like it happened yesterday. Her facial expressions told the story my emotions could not comprehend. I was dealing with something no one was equipped to handle, until it happened to you, and then it became part of life. I had no choice but to dig down deep and find the inner strength I needed to get me through.

For her part, Nancy just nodded and listened, and when she did speak, she said, "I'm sorry, Amy. I'm really sorry."

Mom's crisis occurred because of an untreated mental health condition. For as long as I could remember, Mom had the capability to work forty hours a week, stay up all night sewing clothes, clean the house, visit relatives, and take care of her four girls and our cousin Bonnie, who also lived with us. Sometimes this excessive energy and lack of sleep resulted in high levels of irritability. As a child, I learned to monitor her moods, and go play outside to run off my own energy and anxiety.

When you look at the symptoms of bipolar disorder, her early symptoms were textbook hypomanic and manic. High levels of energy, lack of sleep, irritability, changes in mood, and eventual escalation to a full-blown psychotic break. On the other end, there were depressive symptoms, including sleeping too much, feeling sad for no reason, gaining weight, isolating herself from others, and severe headaches. Without having any awareness that these mood swings had a name and a cause, we just thought it was her "normal" personality.

My father was a man of few words, so we seldom talked about Mom's moods. But he did get me out of the house frequently, taking me with him on many outings. It's because of him that I learned such a great appreciation for the outdoors and sports. As it turned out, sports became my outlet and healthy coping mechanism. Sports came with a built-in support system of coaches and teammates who helped me make it through difficult times.

After only three months of recovery, Mom returned to work full-time.

"It was extremely difficult, and it took me a lot longer to do my work. But I stayed with it, and eventually I got better," she told me one evening when we were talking about how strong she was to push herself and return to work.

Ironically, Mom worked as an administrative assistant at the community mental health center. What she didn't know was that she would become an example to me of how to fight your way back to recovery. For all accounts, she had suffered a traumatic event and was diagnosed with a serious mental illness, and her answer was to tough it out and go back to work. There was never any pity party for Esther. She was tough, persistent, and determined she was going to get better and move on with her life. And she did.

The summer of 1984 was also an Olympic year, and Pat Summitt was the U.S. women's basketball coach. Because of my early success in basketball, I had an opportunity to try out for the women's Olympic basketball team. There was no way I would have made that team, but even being invited to a try out was an accomplishment.

The problem was I had no confidence. I went from being a big fish in a small pond to being a little fish in a big pond. I was a high school All-American, but so was everyone else on my team. The competition and expectations were much greater than I anticipated, and quite honestly, I had a hard time adjusting to not being the star of the team. For quite a few years, I had grown accustomed to reading about myself in the newspaper. I expected to score lots of points and grab tons of rebounds. I had grown comfortable being allowed to make mistakes. But playing for one of the premier teams in the nation meant few mistakes were tolerated. If I could not get the job done—play solid defense, put the ball in the hoop—there was someone else waiting for her opportunity to play. Playing time was a precious commodity, and not getting much of it was something I did not adjust well to.

On top of that, I was completely consumed with dealing with the stress of loving someone who was battling mental illness. So, I passed on going to the tryout and assumed my Olympic dreams were over, at least for the time being.

The summer of 1984 was one that would be marked in my memory forever and take many years to heal from. As much as it's traumatic for the person who lives with a mental illness and is hospitalized from a mental health crisis, it is also extraordinarily stressful for the family members. It's devastating to nearly lose someone you love from an accident, but it's equally heartbreaking to temporarily lose a loved one to mental illness.

Other family members were aware of what happened to Mom, but no one talked about it. Some of our relatives would come and visit, while others stayed away. I learned over the years that some people will stand by you no matter what the circumstances, and others will run for cover as soon as you mention mental illness. And it's even worse when a dramatic mental health crisis occurs. The fear of the unknown gets the best of people every time and causes isolation, not only for the ill person, but also for the loved ones who support them.

What we know about bipolar disorder is that if the condition is not treated, it may have a period of remission and a person might return to a "normal" state. However, like chronic physical illnesses, without treatment, the condition will usually get worse or a person will continue to cycle between mania and depression. My mom struggled for over twenty-five years. She would often go for long periods of time with normal moods. Other times she would have nervous breakdowns, as she called them. But I learned these episodes were most often a result of untreated mania. Without a doubt, each time these mental health crises happened, the entire family was impacted.

If I could offer one suggestion to people who may be on the outside looking in, I would say you don't have to have the right words or understand exactly what is going on. You just need to show kindness and compassion. This goes a long way and means the world to those of us who walk with mental illness on a daily basis. Sometimes the difference between feeling alone on the journey and feeling loved and supported comes down to someone asking simple questions like, "How is everything with your mother?" or, "Are you doing okay?"

The worst thing to me was I knew people were aware of what happened, but pretended nothing was wrong. It was beyond awkward silence. It was flat-out weird. I look at mental illness like a physical illness, and if someone's mother had cancer, I would ask if she was doing okay. Let's not discriminate against those who have mental illness and their loved ones who battle with them on the journey.

Chapter 3

Depression, Devastation, and Rebounding

By the fall of 1984, I was back in Knoxville, beginning my sophomore year at the University of Tennessee. Having to focus my mind on my studies and playing basketball was a much-needed distraction. On a visit home one weekend in October, I'd expected Mom to have fully recovered. What I found was a woman who was still struggling and not taking the appropriate medication regimen. She found the side effects too difficult to handle. But without medication, she needed to recover on her own. It would take a lot longer, and a relapse was almost guaranteed to happen.

The impact of Mom's situation on my own mental health was immediate. It started with an inability to concentrate and escalated into a full-blown depressive episode. I couldn't concentrate in basketball practice; I couldn't remember the offenses. The worse I performed, the more pressure I felt, most of which was self-imposed. I hated that I was not living up to expectations. I believed I was a failure.

One evening after the Christmas holidays, I found myself curled up in a fetal position, crying uncontrollably. And the most terrifying thought came into my mind.

"I should just end it all."

I lived near the Tennessee River, and there was a bridge a stone's throw away from my apartment. My plan was to walk onto the bridge and jump. I had never had suicidal thoughts before, but this would not be the last time I struggled.

I called Cindy and told her what I was going through. She said, "You need to go home and be around people who will love and support you." And I agreed.

It was a huge decision because I truly loved Tennessee and adored Pat Summitt. But I was facing an empty coping mechanism toolbox, and I could not see any other way out.

To her credit, Coach Summitt had made an appointment for me to see a psychiatrist on campus after I returned from visiting my mom in the fall. But the very idea of seeing a psychiatrist terrified me. I was paranoid that he would share my inner thoughts with my coaches. What stood out in my mind most significantly was an underlying belief that only "crazy" people saw psychiatrists. In my mind, I believed I was hurting, but I was certainly not crazy. Unknowingly, my self-stigma started when I was twenty years old, and it would be something that caused unimaginable heartache. I had to overcome it to get well.

On January 1, 1985, I left the University of Tennessee. The team was having an intra-squad scrimmage. Everyone was on the court, except me. I was sitting in the Lady Vol basketball locker room at my private locker, staring at my jersey. I looked around the room, knowing it would be the last time I would see my orange and white uniform hanging in that locker.

I walked out on the court. I was nervous, but I had rehearsed what I was going to say. Pat walked up to me and said, "Amy! What are you doing? We have a scrimmage."

I handed her my orange Lady Vol three-ring binder with all the offensive plays inside. "I came to tell you and the team I'm leaving."

"You don't mean that," she protested.

"Oh, yes, I do, Pat."

I was standing in complete disagreement with a woman who had been a monumental figure in my life for many years. She threw up her hands and called to the team, "You all come here. Amy has something she wants to tell you."

I stood in front of the team and said, "I just wanted to tell you, I'm not happy here. I think it's best for the team and me to leave."

"*No, Amy!*" several teammates yelled out, and some started to cry. I stood emotionless, numb from everything I had been through in the past year. I turned and walked through the door.

Pat followed me out and pleaded with me. "Amy, wait! Please don't leave." She sat down on the stairs with tears in her eyes. "Has it really been that bad for you here?"

"No, Pat. It hasn't been bad." I put my hand on her shoulder, then turned away, walked up the steps, and went out the door.

Two weeks later, I enrolled at West Virginia University in Morgantown. The coaches at WVU welcomed me to the basketball team, but according to NCAA rules, I had to sit out a year before I was eligible to play. This meant for the first time since I was nine years old, I would not have a team to identify with. Even though I could participate in practice with a scrimmage squad, I essentially was not part of the team.

Additionally, I did not receive a release from the University of Tennessee, which meant I had to pay for school at West Virginia. When I transferred, Tennessee could choose whether they wanted to allow me to immediately receive scholarship funds from the school I was transferring to. Most schools give releases. It was a standard policy that Tennessee had adopted for all their women's sports. When I transferred, I was in for sticker shock. I remember going to the campus bookstore and looking at a biology book that cost $85. At Tennessee, my books were covered by a scholarship, but now I had to pay for them. I didn't buy the book.

There was a vast difference between campuses, and although the women's basketball team players were accepting, I had not yet developed many friendships. I did have a roommate, Leah, who was super-supportive and encouraged me to get up on the days I lay in my bed feeling hopeless. I scheduled all my classes for late afternoon and early evening, because I knew I was having a hard time getting out of bed. Leah would come in the room with her infectious, positive attitude and start a conversation, and the fact she was not ignoring me made a difference.

Recently, Leah and I connected on Facebook. I'd given her a Tennessee sweatshirt, which she told me after thirty years she still owns, and I couldn't have it back.

I would lie in bed under the green electric blanket my Aunt Mary Francis had given me. The difference in weather between Knoxville and Morgantown was significant enough that I was always cold. It rarely snowed in Tennessee except in the mountains, but in Morgantown it snowed frequently that year. Staying warm under the covers provided me with a physical and emotional comfort that helped me cope with my struggles.

But I had left my closest friends behind in Tennessee. I soon realized what would become a life lesson—people are the most important part of my life journey, and the connections I make with others are what I value most.

My relocation and transfer resulted in a deeper depression that left me barely able to get out of bed. As much as people were kind to me, they didn't really know me. I was a stranger, and because of this I became extremely isolated for about four months. Even though the suicidal thoughts went away, I was still left with the escalating emotional toll I had experienced in less than a year and a longing in my heart for the dreams that were shattered.

Being closer to home was helpful, but I didn't go home as much as I thought I would. I didn't have a lot of money and I had no close friends. My Tennessee teammates were not only friends, they were like family, and leaving them left me with a big hole in my heart.

To keep myself busy, I would find my way to the recreation center on campus where the guys were playing basketball. I tried to play with them a couple of times, but I had no energy or interest. Eventually, I stopped going to the rec center because I found it very depressing.

What started to help change my mood was my random encounter with a guy from my hometown. I was wandering around the coliseum (the basketball facility) one day, looking in the windows of the racquetball courts. I tapped on one door, and Jim opened it.

I said, "Do you want to play a game?"

"Sure," he said, kind of laughing.

After he lost five games, he decided to tell me his name and where he was from. We discovered we went to the same high school, though we did not know each other. This was the start of a friendship that would last several years.

Racquetball turned out to be one of the key factors that helped lift my depressive mood. Looking back, it wasn't so much the sport, although exercise does help depression, it was the friendships I gained that made all the difference in my mental health.

Shortly after I met Jim, I met Bill, who worked at the coliseum as a security guard. His shift ended at 11:00 p.m. He would let me in the building, and we would play until 2:00 a.m. My classes were late in the day, so I could sleep in the next morning. Between Jim and Bill, they kept me really busy.

One characteristic which has always worked for me is my innate ability to never give up. This sheer determination, combined with the effects of underlying bipolar disorder and a foundational upbringing of faith in God, pulled me out of my depression and set me on my way to breathing life back into my dreams.

In one of my toughest moments, I recalled a conversation I'd had with my sister Shelley as we watched the 1984 summer Olympics.

I said, "I know I'm a good enough athlete to make the Olympic team. I don't know what sport I can play, but I know I'll find one and become an Olympian one day."

Shelley tells me she doesn't remember the conversation, but I will never forget it. It was about seeing the dream. Believing what could be possible. This trait would become the fuel that powered me through my recovery journey.

From the fall in Tennessee to the spring in West Virginia, I had gone through a difficult period of depression. I did not have a name for my symptoms, but looking back, I am able to identify the patterns of my behavior as a depressive episode. For me, this included lack of energy, no motivation to do the things I enjoyed, a decrease in concentration, and sleeping hours but never feeling rested…and sometimes the dreaded suicidal thoughts. These symptoms dogged me for months.

I finally began to feel like myself again by the time the school year was about to end. My confidence was coming back, and I was making new friends. I recalled a conversation I'd had with my friend Joe Smith, who was a sports writer from New York. I had been playing basketball in the Olympic Sports Festival in Indianapolis while I was a junior in high school. He took me to see this sport called team handball.

While we were watching the game and he was explaining how it was played, he told me, "One day, after you're finished playing basketball, you should try handball. I think you'd be very good at it."

As a side note, team handball (also known as team handball, Olympic handball, European team handball, or European handball) is a sport in which two teams of seven players each, six court players and a goalkeeper, pass a ball using their hands with the aim of throwing it into the goal of the other team. A standard match consists of two periods of thirty minutes, and the team that scores the most goals wins. Think of it as a cross between basketball and soccer with your hands. Team handball has been an Olympic sport since 1972 for the men, and 1976 for the women. It's not as popular in the United States as it is in other countries around the world.

The U.S. Olympic Sports Festival began in 1978 and ended in 1995. It was the largest amateur multi-sport event held in the United States by the U.S. Olympic Committee in the years between Olympic Games. I had landed a spot on the East team for women's basketball through a tryout my junior year in high school. I was one of the youngest players in the country to make the team. This gave me national exposure as an up-and-coming young women's basketball player.

Toward the end of the semester at WVU, I had this idea to call the Team Handball Federation to see if I could try out for one of their Olympic Sports Festival teams. The idea really came from two seeds planted in my mind. One was from the conversation I'd had with my friend Joe, and the second was from having already participated in two Olympic Sports Festivals in women's basketball. That was why I was qualified to try out for the 1984 Olympic women's basketball team.

I made the phone call and found out where they were having the handball tryouts. I traveled to Johnstown, Pennsylvania and Charleston, West Virginia, for a couple of sessions. They invited me to join a club team and travel to Colorado Springs for a National Team Handball tournament.

After playing in the tournament, I was selected to play in the 1985 Olympic Sports Festival in Baton Rouge, Louisiana. My family was happy for me despite not understanding how handball was played. But they knew it was something I wanted to do, so they supported me. At least until I phoned from Baton Rouge and told Mom I had been chosen to join the National Team Handball training team. Which I followed up with, "I'm going to quit school and go with the team to train in Marquette, Michigan."

Needless to say, this was not a well-received phone call. But I had the element of strong-minded behavior—which, translated, said I was going to do what I wanted because it was my life. Admittedly, some of my assertions in making my own decisions were attributed to temporarily being unable to rely on my mom for decision-making help. At the end of the day, I was going to make my own choices about my life's direction, and that included a dream to become an Olympic athlete. No one was going to stand in my way going down that path, and no bout with depression was going to stop me.

I also dealt with a number of people who told me if I quit school, I would never finish college. What they didn't know was I had spent my life proving people wrong, so this was simply more motivation to push myself harder and achieve my dreams.

When it was all said and done, I participated in five Olympic Sports Festivals—two in women's basketball and three in team handball. I collected a tremendous amount of great memories and good friendships.

In the summer before I left for the team handball training camp, I took a job as a Domino's pizza driver. I saved all my money to buy a very expensive Fuji road bicycle. I would use that bike for years, including riding over 100 miles in the El Tour De Tucson annual ride. I grew up with a mother who believed "if there's a will, there's a way." I learned if I wanted something, it was almost always within my grasp. I just had to work for it. Later in life, these experiences would help me with my recovery journey.

* * *

The phone rang one evening two weeks before I was scheduled to leave for Michigan, and it was a heart-wrenching call. I had been packing my bags and getting ready to leave when I answered the phone to find a social worker from a hospital in Baltimore on the other end of the line.

"Is this the residence of Sherry Gamble's mother, Esther?"

"Yes, it is." Cold chills ran up the back of my legs. *What's wrong now?*

"I'm calling from the psychiatric hospital…"

I handed the phone to my mother. I was so emotionally distraught, I ran out of the house. I thought, "Here we go again. Another crazy situation we'll all have to deal with." Suddenly, all the emotion from the past year exploded like a dam breaking, and nothing could stop the emotions from flowing. Without really knowing what was wrong with Sherry, I assumed the worst. It was a domino effect in my mind, and having been through the trauma with my mother made me a bit on edge.

A handball teammate, Sheri, was visiting with us at the time, and she came outside to comfort me. My father was telling me to calm down. All I could think of was how "crazy" my family had become in such a short time. I ran through the front yard and punched a tree. Sheri grabbed my hand and held me while I cried.

Sheri kept saying, "It's okay, Amy. It's going to be okay."

Choking back my tears and shivering, I sputtered out, "I can't take any more."

A flood of tears and indescribable pain—deep, emotional pain—oozed from my pores. I was only twenty years old and had now dealt with three mental health crisis situations in about a year. How could one person endure so much?

Imagine seeing the world through the eyes of a young adult about to realize a childhood dream, when suddenly, all the characters she's surrounded by lose their sanity. How do you even begin to explain these things to people you meet along the way? I would have to learn how to answer that question over time.

But I learned a very valuable lesson. It was not all about me. That Mom and Sherry had experienced a mental health crisis was not a direct reflection upon myself. It would take a few years before I experienced my own mental health crisis, and those experiences are not a direct reflection on my family either.

I don't know how long Sherry stayed in the hospital, but she received a diagnosis of bipolar disorder and would continue to struggle for quite some time. She ended up in the frequent flyer program of various psychiatric hospitals. Usually, she was never kept long enough to get stable. At one point, she left a hospital and drove to the Baltimore airport. She parked her car curbside and took off on a flight to Germany. No one knew where she was going. We only found out when the State Department called my parents' home. She was admitted to a psychiatric hospital in Germany.

My father had taken the phone call from the State Department. "Well, Sherry's managed to find her way on the

State Department's radar. What's next?" he commented as he retold the story to the rest of the family.

We later learned she had been abducted on a train and beaten up by thugs taking advantage of a vulnerable person. It was the first time she crossed paths with dangerous people, but it would not be the last.

I had learned to block out all the high drama, and I became very adept in handling crisis situations involving bipolar disorder. While Sherry was getting treatment in a foreign country, I began my training with the team handball national team and started a three-year journey to become an Olympian.

Chapter 4

Let The Games Begin

In 1985, after spending three months training in Marquette, Michigan, the U.S. team handball national team went to Europe for the World Championships. One great advantage of handball not being a popular sport in the U.S. was it gave us the opportunity to travel internationally for competitive matches. By the time I was twenty-two years old, I had visited over eighteen countries around the world. It opened my eyes to so many different cultures, and traveling was one of my greatest teachers.

One particular trip was strikingly memorable. We had gone to Russia to train and play top-notch competition. Between matches, we went sightseeing, and we went to Red Square in Moscow to visit Lenin's Tomb. The body of Vladimir Lenin has been on public display in the mausoleum since 1924. Saying it's a special place would not do justice to how important it is to the Russian people.

We descended a staircase and walked in silence around the glass tomb containing Lenin's body. As I walked toward the structure, I put my hands in my pockets, not knowing that was forbidden while inside the mausoleum. Instantly, Russian guards came running toward me with machine guns, screaming, "No!" Apparently, they thought I might have something destructive in my pocket. I later 'fessed up to my teammates that I was terrified and thought I was going to be shot. They all thought it was funny.

I also had times when living the dream put me front and center with adversity, such as when I came in contact with and was bitten by a brown recluse spider and had to have emergency surgery in a small hospital in Kamen, Germany. I didn't speak the language and didn't have an interpreter with me. The only thing I remember the nurse telling me was, "You poor dear. We must to cut!"

I only had a few German coins, but I had enough to call my sister Cindy.

"Cindy, I'm in the hospital in Germany. They're telling me I need surgery on my arm. It's infected from a spider bite. The red streaks are running up my arm. It feels like an egg stuck in my arm. I'm scared." I rattled quickly, one statement running into the next.

Cindy remained calm. "You have to let them do the surgery or you could lose your arm. Tell them to give you a local anesthetic."

"What's a local?" I asked. And suddenly the phone clicked off. I had run out of money.

I walked back into the hospital waiting room, and they called me in for emergency surgery. I was lying on the table being prepped when they started to put a mask over my face.

"Wait!" I said loudly. "Can I have a local?"

The surgeon laughed and in his broken English said, "You must to go to sleep now and have big, beautiful dreams of walking the beach."

When I woke up from the surgery, they were putting a plaster cast on my arm. I was wheeled outside to a hallway on a small gurney that was barely big enough for me. The hallway was dark and no one was around. Apparently, the small community hospital did not have enough rooms.

After a little while, my teammates Portia and Lisa showed up at the hospital and told me they were springing me out. The nurse didn't say anything when I asked for my clothes. I am pretty sure she spoke very little English.

We took a taxi back to the hotel where the team was staying, and the next morning we left on a long train ride for Switzerland. My arm was throbbing. I had no pain medication, antibiotics, not even a Tylenol. I had no idea what was under that cast.

After we arrived at the hotel in Switzerland, Rita, one of the assistant coaches, came to my room and told me they would take me to the hospital the next morning.

I said, "But my arm really hurts. It's throbbing."

"Well, the coaches decided you'll go in the morning," Rita said like it was no big deal.

She left, and I proceeded to have a fit. There was a stack of glass ashtrays on the table outside my room. I picked up an ashtray and threw it, shattering little pieces all over the floor and prompting my teammates to come running to my rescue.

Eventually, that evening, Rita and I took a taxi to the nearest hospital. I heard through the grapevine that everyone thought I was being a baby. I was overreacting and emotional.

After waiting in the emergency room for a little while, the nurse called my name. Rita said, "I'll be waiting for you out here. If you need me, tell them to come get me." I walked back into a room with several beds next to each other without any curtains.

The doctor came over and asked me a few questions in his broken English. He said, "We will have to remove the cast. I'm going to cut it in two pieces, so we can put it back on." I didn't say one word.

He cut the cast off and began removing the gauze. Everything was fine and I was very calm until he started to pull the gauze out of a hole in my arm the size of a fifty-cent piece. The flesh, blood, and yellow pus was oozing out of my arm, and I heaved as if I were going to vomit.

I cried out, "Go get my coach, please."

"Stop crying or I am not going to treat you!" the doctor ordered.

The nurse went and got Rita from the waiting room, and when she came around the corner, her face turned white when she saw the open wound in my arm.

It was the last time anyone called me a baby.

At every turn in my life, I was challenged with all forms and shapes of adversity. As the saying goes, "That which does not kill us makes us stronger." People have told me God has a plan for me, and I was given the strength to endure so I could one day use my experiences to do something good and help other people. I believe they're right.

In January 1986, the team moved to Colorado Springs to the Olympic Training Center. We became resident athletes and would live there for the next two and a half years. It was at this time that I mark my calendar retrospectively with symptoms of hypomania, a mild form of mania and marked by elation and hyperactivity.

As a team, we trained for about eight hours a day, but while my teammates were resting, I would find some other activity to participate in—like a friendly game or five of racquetball with one of the men's team handball players, a bike ride of forty or fifty miles, or simply an extra two- or three-mile run. I had so much excess energy at times, I had to keep moving.

At the other end of the bipolar spectrum, there were times when I had difficulty getting out of bed. All I wanted to do was sleep, but somehow I managed to drag myself to practice. A day in the life of an athlete living with undiagnosed and untreated bipolar disorder.

To be honest, knowing how medications for bipolar disorder affect me, I don't think I would have become an Olympian if I had been taking them. There is far too much weight gain, lethargy, and other side effects that would have made it nearly impossible for me to train and play sports. What was happening at that time was my ability to manage my symptoms with exercise. And it worked for a while.

In June 1986, the team went to Sweden seeking to play high level competition. We were given an option of not going to Sweden because the Chernobyl Nuclear Disaster in the Ukraine, which was part of the former Soviet Union, had happened a couple months prior. There was evidence radioactive material had made its way to Sweden, but no one on the team opted to forego the trip, though we joked when we saw gigantic jackrabbits on our runs through the woods. We called them "radiation rabbits."

I had a terrible time adjusting to the sun shining in the wee morning hours. From early May until late August, the sun sets around midnight and rises again at about four in the morning in Sweden.

I would wake up in the middle of the night and sneak out of the house. Carrying my piano music, as I often did, I would find my way to an open gym and play the piano for hours. I'm not sure why there was a piano in the gym, but I believe it was a multi-source center where other events took place besides sports.

I don't remember ever being tired the next day. Perhaps my illness stayed in check because of all the training we were doing—three times a day practices and long runs to keep us in shape. It turned out to be a healthy way for me to manage an onset of bipolar disorder.

We were staying on a Swedish island in the Baltic Sea. We swore it was a weight loss camp, stereotypically called a "fat farm." Everyone on the team lost weight in the nearly ten days we stayed there. We weren't allowed to eat the meat, eggs, or milk because of the potential radiation contamination. There were no grocery stores to be found. We either ate what they gave us or starved. That is, until one day when Lisa and I discovered a snack shop on the other side of the hill. We snuck down and bought cookies, soda, and candy. It made our time in isolation tolerable.

When the trip to Sweden was coming to an end, a few teammates and I borrowed the van one evening. Someone had managed to confiscate the keys. We crept out of the hotel, put the van in neutral, and pushed it until we were at a safe distance to start it up so our coaches couldn't hear.

I am really not sure why we did it. All we did was drive around Stockholm and go into a 7-Eleven store. I don't even think anyone drank any alcohol on that outing. We never got caught by the coaches.

In July 1986, the team traveled to Moscow for the 1986 Goodwill Games. The games were developed by Ted Turner, from the Turner Broadcasting Network, as a response to the Olympic boycotts in 1980 by the United States and 1984 by the former Soviet Union. Approximately 3000 athletes from

79 nations participated. The Soviet Union dominated the medal count. I don't know if we even won one game. The team was still in the early stages of development and we hadn't quite become competitive.

One of the nice things about the entire team handball traveling experiences was the coaches and managers always took us to other cultural events. We went to see a Russian opera. It was the first time I had ever seen an opera. Even though I could not understand the language, I was mesmerized by the intense emotions of the performers. It was fascinating.

We also had an opportunity to visit a Russian museum, where I took a picture of a display of an American housewife. It was an overweight female wax figure with her hair in old-fashioned pink plastic curlers, with a cigarette hanging out of her mouth. She was pushing a shopping cart overflowing with TV dinners and canned goods. My, what a message that display was sending to those who visited the museum.

In addition to our trips overseas, we managed to have lots of fun in Colorado Springs. During a weekend we had off from training, a group of us decided to go whitewater rafting. It was springtime, and the water was rushing.

There were eight of us in the raft, including the guide. It was a time before helmets were commonly worn. All of us had shorts on, even though it was not exactly shorts weather in the mountains. The water was frigid.

All was going well until the raft hit an unexpected whirlpool rapid. The guide was thrown from the back of the raft to the front, knocking everyone on the right side out of the raft. Our teammate Sam Jones was in the front and was spared. It was a good thing, because she could not swim.

I was one who found myself getting twisted and pulled through the mighty rapids. I was smart enough to cover my head with my hands. I kept calm and went with the flow, all while my knees were scraping the rocks, and the whitewater rapids dragged me downstream.

I held my breath for as long as I could, finally reaching calm waters. I quickly tried to come to the aid of my teammates, but above my head was the raft. I struggled with my right arm and pulled myself to the edge of the raft. As soon as he saw my head, the guide pulled me up into the boat, with the force of the water pulling my all-in-one, green Adidas shorts down to my ankles. I didn't care because I was freezing, scared, and happy to be alive.

Portia screamed, "A-my! We thought you were dead. Holy shit, that was scary."

I said nothing while each person took turns telling their version of the story. I sat with knees clenched and my feet jammed under the seat in front of me for the remainder of the trip. Those of us who were tossed over the side were all freezing. All I wanted to do was crawl into my bed under my nice warm blankets. Not surprisingly, I have never gone whitewater rafting again.

* * *

It is highly unlikely for a girl from Sherrard, West Virginia to become an Olympian, let alone an Olympic team handball player. Additionally, I had to overcome more than my share of tough situations. But my path in life led me all the way to the 1988 Summer Olympics in Seoul, South Korea. Even though I was dealing with my own mental health challenge and the emotionally demanding situation with my mom and sister, I persevered in the face of extreme challenges.

Not only did I have to deal with the background of Mom's and Sherry's mental illness challenges, I also had several injuries. Shortly after I recovered from the spider bite, I was riding double on a bicycle with my teammate Portia. I was joking around, and before I knew it, we had hit the ground with Portia falling on top of me. I ended up with a cracked clavicle and a torn rotator cuff.

My life had started to shape up in patterns. Things would go well for a while, and then something bad would happen.

Get better. Heal. Repeat. Everything was spinning like a washing machine that would not shut off. After healing from the rotator cuff, I broke a bone in my foot. I would lose my position on the team then have to work my way back into the starting lineup. I became accustomed to coping with disappointment followed by a great sense of satisfaction knowing I had rebounded.

On one occasion, we were playing an inter-squad scrimmage in Denver. I jumped in the air to make a pass, and one of my teammates collided with me. On impact, my kneecap was dislocated. My friend Bruce, who came to watch us play, took me to the emergency room.

The doctor walked in and said, "Show me the woman who has the thirty-eight beats per minute heart rate." This was followed by, "Take it again. I don't believe it's true."

The nurse took my pulse again. Same thing.

"Why do you have such a low heart rate?"

"I'm training for the Olympics." After he learned this information, he understood how it could be possible. An athlete at this level of conditioning would have a very low resting heart rate.

I had two knee injuries, one of which was the extremely painful dislocated kneecap. But always, I picked myself back up and kept on fighting. My focus was on achieving the dream. While adversity in my life was a pattern, so was fighting back. I was shaping the way I would handle future struggles, and I was building resiliency.

This is why I wholeheartedly believe in speaking to young people about overcoming obstacles. I have lived through circumstances that have given me the experience to believe people can defeat even the greatest of odds.

* * *

In September 1988, we left the Olympic Training Center in Colorado Springs and headed for Los Angeles, where we would receive our Olympic gear. They took us to a big tent and gave us a shopping cart. It was like going shopping, except there was no charge for all the cool gear, gadgets, and Olympic pins.

After we were outfitted, the next day we all went to Disneyland for an official send-off. It was so cool to ride on the float with Mickey, Minnie Mouse, and many of the other Disney characters. We waved to all the cheering folks who had lined the streets of Disneyland to watch the evening parade. It was the first event, putting an exclamation point on the fact we were about to accomplish something extraordinary. We were treated like VIPs and announced as Olympians. Disneyland even gave us a commemorative medal marking the date and time of our parade appearance.

It wasn't the first time as an athlete I had received special treatment. When I participated in the Olympic Sports Festivals in my junior and senior years of high school, I had a taste on a smaller scale of what was to come. When I played at Tennessee, we very often received special treatment by the fans and boosters. Making it to the Final Four was an incredible experience. We stayed in Beverly Hills, California and were given some great one-of-a-kind athletic gear. Looking back, all my past athletic experiences were preparing me for the grand stage.

The day of opening ceremonies, about ten thousand athletes from around the world were bussed to a holding area hours before the Olympic opening ceremonies began. Our uniform was a long sleeve white blouse, light blue sweater, white skirt, and white pumps. It might go down in history as one of the ugliest opening ceremonies outfits ever! To make matters worse, the weather was scorching hot. We all took off our sweaters and wrapped them around our waist as we waited in a football sized arena to be let into Olympic Stadium.

It was a very festive atmosphere, with lots of laughter and excitement. Everyone was taking pictures. I walked through the crowd of athletes and found my Russian team handball friends. I took a picture with Carl Lewis, the world class track athlete. I also had some photos taken with Bridgett Gordon, a women's basketball player who I helped recruit at the University of Tennessee. There were athletes who I had admired from afar, and then I was standing with them all for this event that would be viewed all over the globe.

By the time we finally entered Olympic Stadium, night had fallen. We all had American flags, and we had jokingly practiced our parade wave. So many cameras were flashing. It looked like a gazillion fireflies in a field of dreams. I was in awe. Here I was, this country girl from Sherrard, West Virginia, standing on one of the biggest stages in the world. I was overwhelmed with the grand nature of the Olympic Games, and it took several years before my accomplishment would actually sink in.

One of the greatest memories I have is from the Olympic opening ceremony. Standing on the floor of the stadium, I looked up into the stands filled with seventy thousand people and picked out Mom in the crowd. I can't remember how I knew what section she was sitting in. But I wasn't the only American standing in the middle of the field, out of the official lineup, jumping up and down waving. I believe the Korean media called us *"unruly Americans."*

Mom had made the trip to Seoul to see her youngest daughter walk in the parade of athletes. After what she had been through three years prior, it was beyond words what I felt about her surviving and thriving again. No doubt, a real-life blessing. Her trip was made possible by Seagram's Coolers Send the Family Members Program. The company gave an all-expense paid trip for one family member of every Olympic athlete, more than five hundred people. Turned out Seagram's wanted to be an official sponsor of the Olympic team, but was told "no" by the Olympic Committee. Something about "whiskey" not representing the greatest image for Olympians.

* * *

Opening ceremonies is a celebration for the athletes, but is also an opportunity for the host country to showcase their culture to the world. The choreography of all the young Korean women dancing in perfect synchronicity is etched in my memory. The lighting of the Olympic flame brought tears to my eyes. And finally, the thundering celebration of thousands of people started when we all heard the words, *"Let the games begin!"*

Our handball coach would not allow us to attend other events until our competition was over, but Mom had the chance to see history being made in other sports, like diving and tennis. She got to see Olympic diver Greg Louganis win a gold medal. It was a historical moment, because he had taken a dive and hit his head on the platform before landing in the pool. He managed to regain his composure and win an Olympic gold medal.

I was especially cheering for Greg because we had crossed paths at the Olympics. One afternoon we had visited one of the shopping areas and were about to board a van to head back to Olympic Village. All my teammates were crammed in, and I had the only open seat beside me. Greg poked his head in the van and asked for a ride back to the Village. Everyone was moving over making room for him, and I just kind of sat there. He came and sat by me, and we talked all the way back.

A few days later, I was having breakfast in the cafeteria when he asked if he could sit with me. There is always a pecking order in our society, and the Olympics are no exception. There are the high-profile athletes…and then the rest of us. Of course, Greg was high profile and everyone knew who he was. I remember walking back with Greg to the condo where the handball team was staying. As Greg and I were talking, a group of the men's team handball squad walked past us.

They all yelled, "Hi, Greg!" with excitement.

One person said, "Oh, hey, Amy."

They were all looking at me, wondering why Greg Louganis was walking with me!

Competing in the Olympics was surreal. We had a talented squad and had managed to become a respected team in the world. But looking back, it is easy to see we were over-trained. By the time the competition came, we were tired. I said to one of my teammates in our first game, "Do your legs feel like lead?" I knew mine did.

In a whirlwind of a summer, we had spent weeks traveling in Europe, including another trip to Russia. We were only back in Colorado Springs for about ten days before we left for Los Angeles then headed to Seoul. When we got to Seoul, we trained for ten days before the Olympics even started. I don't know if all my teammates would agree, but we were tired.

We finished seventh out of eight teams. Korea won both the men's and women's gold medals. But what some people don't realize is that in order to get to the Olympics, we had to qualify. Not every team in the world competes in the Olympics, so it is an accomplishment just to get there. I would have loved to have a won a medal, but that was not in the cards.

My mom and I got together a few times. She came to all the games and took lots of pictures. She had met up with some friends who lived in Korea and really got to explore the countryside. No one would have known she had been through hell just three years ago.

When the Olympics were over, several members of the team and I made a side trip to Hawaii. One evening we were watching a television special showing highlights from the Games and the closing ceremony. At the Games, while I was watching the extinguishing of the Olympic flame, a cameraman had stood in front of me for quite some time. When my face landed across the screen for several seconds, my teammates started yelling at me to wake up and look at the TV. I sat up and said, "Oh, yeah, I guess it is me." Years later, a friend gave me an Olympic highlight tape with that frame of me in it. A true gift to remember those moments.

I never let myself get overly excited about too many things. I believe it had to do with my upbringing and culture. I learned humility and how to be humble, so much so that it appeared I was not confident. My confidence was held close to my heart, and sometimes, on the surface, other people didn't see it. Part of building more confidence comes from acknowledging achievements, and that was never something I was especially skilled at. When I faced the biggest challenge of my life, I would have to learn how to build self-esteem and confidence from the ground up, and that meant I would have to rely on some of my past successes to fuel my recovery.

During my time playing team handball, I had the opportunity to learn in so many ways. I remember the time I set out from our hotel in Sao Paulo, Brazil, and I walked the streets in shock at how differently people lived. On the hillside where the hotel was, there was running water and inside bathrooms. Down the hill, people did not have running water or a house foundation. I saw one house where the mud was equal with the front door. It made an incredible impression on how I viewed America and made me realize how fortunate I was to live there.

One of my coaches was from Budapest, Hungary, so we spent a significant time in that country. I learned how upset the people were at the Russians who invaded their country in World War II. My coach was a young boy when that happened, and he still held deep resentment. We had spent several weeks with the Russian team traveling to various U.S. cities, including my hometown, and I became friends with many of the Russian handball players. I was a starter on the team, and my coach benched me one game.

He said, "Why must you be friends with these people? They destroyed my country."

I held my ground and replied, "These young women had nothing to do with what happened in World War II. They weren't even born yet."

He looked at me with disgust. But I knew even if I did not change his mind, I had made him think.

We spent weeks in Sweden and Denmark on multiple occasions. I learned in those places women go topless when sunbathing. When the Swedish team came to Colorado Springs to play in a tournament, someone had to tell them in our society you can't sunbathe topless unless you are in a special place. It was very eye-opening to learn the differences in cultures.

In Colorado Springs at the Olympic Training Center, our basic necessities were taken care of—food, uniforms, travel expenses—but anything extra we had to buy ourselves. I was among the fortunate ones who had Mercantile Bank from my hometown who sponsored me. My Aunt Mary Francis was also very generous and sent me checks every week. Some of my teammates would come and hang out with my roommate Portia and me because we had the only VCR, and I had the means to rent movies and buy snacks.

But the big sponsorship came when my mother wrote a letter responding to an article in a newsletter from my father's health insurance provider, Blue Cross/Blue Shield. They wanted to sponsor three athletes training for the Olympics who were children of federally employed beneficiaries. My dad had been working for the federal government for many years.

Much to everyone's surprise, I was selected as one of the athletes they would sponsor. This meant an all-expense paid trip to Washington, D.C. for me, and lunch with the program administrators. I remember sitting at an outdoor restaurant on K Street having lunch and being surrounded by people dressed in business attire. I never felt out of place in situations I found myself in; I just kind of went with the flow. At some level, I realized not everyone had the opportunity to have these types of experiences, but I never spent much time thinking about it.

When I look back on the many wonderful experiences being a team handball Olympian afforded me, it's still the relationships with other people that matter most. We made lifelong memories together, and even in my very open struggles with bipolar disorder, I have remained friends with the people I was closest to.

One of my dear friends, Meg, stayed in close contact for several years. She became a women's college basketball coach, and I often made a point of watching her team play. We hiked the Grand Canyon together a couple of times with a group of friends. When I moved back to the East Coast, it became more difficult to maintain a close friendship, but I still keep in touch through Facebook. She has been a person who never judged me for my challenges and struggles with bipolar disorder.

My friend Sheri Winn and I keep up with Facebook as well. She became a women's college basketball coach at several different schools and landed at the University of Charleston in West Virginia. She is now an extremely successful author and motivational speaker and lives in Montana. She has encouraged me to write this book and forge onward with my own speaking career.

One of the best handball players in U.S. history is the director of the Olympic Alumni Association. She has been nothing but supportive of me over the years. Anytime I was giving a speech, I could call Cindy Stinger, and she would send me a care package of Olympic pins and stickers to give the kids. I could always count on Cindy.

There are so many other examples of people I have met along the way. After living together for three years, it is a bond that stands the test of time. We accomplished a goal together that many can only dream about, and yet we lived it. Time may march on, but the memories will live forever.

Chapter 5

Basketball and Big Decisions

The Olympics finished in October 1988, just in time for me to move on to my next challenge—going back to college and playing Division I women's college basketball. While most of my handball teammates headed to Washington, D.C. to meet President Reagan on the White House lawn, I headed to Tucson to play basketball and finish college at the University of Arizona. I've never been good at celebrating accomplishments or being recognized, but I do regret not going to the White House, a once in a lifetime opportunity.

The Olympics ended in October, which meant the school year had already started, but the NCAA gave Olympians a waiver which said we could compete with our teams without being enrolled in classes. There would have been no way to make up two months of class work. This gave me the opportunity to transition my way back into college basketball without having to go to class. It was fun while it lasted.

After I transferred from Tennessee, I still had eligibility to play NCAA basketball, but I had to complete my eligibility within five years after I played my first game. Except, I received a sixth year because I had participated in the Olympics, an exception to the rule. In short, I was a twenty-three-year-old senior.

My mom and dad had lived in Tucson in the 1950s. My dad was in the Air Force and stationed at Davis-Monthan Air Force Base. They lived there for two years then returned to West Virginia.

Some people believe in fate, and some believe in miracles. I have had far too many mysterious situations to not believe in the latter. Life is all about the connections we weave, and my life experience takes that concept to an entirely different level. One of the assistant coaches from Arizona, Kirsten, had tried out for the team handball national team during the time I was in Colorado Springs. We'd had a conversation about basketball, and I'd mentioned I had some eligibility remaining and that I had played a year and a half at Tennessee. When she returned to Arizona, she discussed me with assistant coach June Olkowski.

June had recruited me in high school when she was an assistant coach at the University of Maryland. She remembered me and called within a short time. June said, "I'm not the head coach, so I can't make you any promises, but I want to let you know we're interested in the possibility of you playing for us."

As luck would have it, June became the head coach at the University of Arizona. I happened to have a speaking engagement in Tucson with Blue Cross/Blue Shield, my corporate sponsor, so we visited and I took a tour of the campus. I made a verbal commitment to play at Arizona.

I gave my first official speech at the Loew's Ventana Resort. At the base of the Tucson mountains with virgin desert and starry skies, it was a precursor to the life ahead of me in corporate America. I even had a speech writer and used a teleprompter. I can't remember a thing I said, but I know I was comfortable in front of a crowd. My voice never quivered and my legs didn't shake, which is half the battle in public speaking.

* * *

My mental health was stable during my first year at Arizona. I became a First Team All-Conference player and led the team in scoring and rebounding. I was only allowed to play one season because the NCAA would not give me a waiver. My second year at Arizona I spent in school taking twenty-five to twenty-eight credit hours a semester in my attempt to graduate as quickly as possible. Most people take a maximum of eighteen hours. I was really pushing the limits.

Ultimately, I only played two and a half years of college basketball, losing one and a half years because I had transferred to other schools and had opted to train for the Olympics. As far as academics were concerned, I graduated in fewer than four years of attendance. I could often lose myself in studying and found a great deal of confidence in the classroom. To me, reading and learning have a very therapeutic value.

There were many people who said I would never graduate from college if I quit school to pursue my Olympic dreams. I've learned that if you are going to follow your heart, you can't worry about what the critics say. Predictions about someone else's life are better left unsaid. I also learned that I was developing a pretty good compass on making decisions and taking risks other people might find excessive. But that has always been my nature. I can look back and say, "I made mistakes along the way, but I can't blame anyone else for my decisions." I took the phrase "go for it" to new heights.

Even though I had a heavy course load, I still managed to have lots of fun. To manage my stress, I ran about three miles every morning. If my roommate and former teammate Greta was looking for me, she knew I was either on a fifty-mile bike ride or running somewhere in the desert. She was a great friend who always had my best interest at heart.

My friend Jim, who I had met at WVU, had challenged me to participate in the El Tour de Tucson, a 106-mile ride around the city. I began training religiously in my spare time.

During a training ride on my bike, I was caught in a major storm about twenty miles outside of Tucson. I quickly learned the meaning of "monsoon." I could see the storm as I rode from the sunny mountains down to the valley. I was relentlessly pedaling into the wicked wind, and I felt skin-pinching raindrops pierce through my shirt, as if I were being beaten. The sky had pitch-black clouds and lightning that came out of nowhere, cracking all around me. I persistently pedaled directly into the storm. Finally, I made it home safely, and a few months later I rode across the finish line and completed my first and last El Tour de Tucson.

At the end of the school year, I was asked to play team handball in the Olympic Sports Festival in Oklahoma City. I decided to play, even though I was pretty certain my sports career was coming to an end.

During the opening ceremonies, President Reagan came to speak with all the athletes. I had been using sign language to talk with another athlete who was deaf, and she asked me to join her right next to the stage, so she could see the interpreters. When President Reagan left the stage, the secret service hurried him through the roped-off crowd. I was literally three feet from him when his eyes met mine. I had always heard about his majestic blue eyes, but seeing them in person put an exclamation point on them. Since I didn't get to meet him after the Olympics, it was kind of cool being that close to him.

My team won the gold medal at the festival. It was a great experience, but a bit of a letdown after being in the Olympics. I've learned it is nearly impossible to surpass the Olympic Games.

During the 1989-1990 season, I still attended all the basketball games, even though I was no longer playing. I was surprised during one game when a radio commentator asked me if I wanted to provide "color commentating." I had no idea what I was doing, but he invited me to come down to the station and practice. I spent the remainder of the season doing commentating, even though I don't believe I was very good at it.

After I graduated, Mom came to Tucson for a visit and to celebrate my accomplishment. She and I went to the Grand Canyon and hiked the Bright Angel Trail to and from the Colorado River Overlook. It was twelve miles in one day, and she made it at fifty-five years old. I highly doubt I could do that hike at age fifty-five, but I'm sure going to try. She is an extraordinary woman. Despite her challenges with bipolar disorder, Mom and I always managed to create some very special memories.

In 1990, at the end of what became my senior year in college, I had three options. One was to go overseas and play professional basketball in Japan for the Bank of Tokyo. Two was to work for a major pharmaceutical company, and three was to play basketball and obtain a master's degree at Prince Edward Island University in Canada. Canada's athletic association had different rules than the NCAA, so I still had eligibility to play. I never realized at the time how beautiful Prince Edward Island is until I watched the movie *Anne of Green Gables*. Any one of those choices would have been a good decision.

My mental health at the time played a big role in the decision I made. I was leaning toward going to Japan, but I became so depressed I could not motivate myself to work on my game. I had difficulty running around the block, much less running a few miles. I didn't want to get to Japan and not feel well.

My classes ended the first week of July, and by the second week, I was in Arlington, Texas in training with Merck. After three months of training, I moved to Las Vegas, Nevada. I decided working for Merck would be the more "secure" path. Despite ending my athletic career, the transition to corporate America was relatively smooth. In business, there is a significant emphasis on performance, and I love performance objectives. From all accounts, I made the right decision.

Chapter 6

Highs and Lows in Las Vegas

Some people claim one of the worst places to live if you have bipolar disorder is Las Vegas. It's a twenty-four-hour city, and if you have a manic episode, you might get yourself in a heap of trouble or end up with a new husband or two. Fortunately, the worst manic episode I had in Las Vegas resulted in staying up all night then going on a sixteen-mile hike the next day. The thing was, at that point, I didn't know there was anything wrong with me. I thought everyone could do those kinds of things.

What probably saved me from a faster onset of severe illness was my extreme exercising. I ran half-marathons, rode my bike long distances, hiked, and played racquetball several times a week. Of course, I also worked full-time, and that consisted of walking miles per day, as well.

Being in pharmaceutical sales in the 1990s was drastically different than it has become today. The industry was highly respected back then, and Merck was Fortune 500's number one company for five years in a row.

I started out as a sales representative. It was a great place to work, and the training they gave us was phenomenal. When we launched a new product, we would spend an entire week in training learning everything about that product. And the focus was on the patients. We were not all about driving product sales, and the industry had not quite evolved into the evil empire it has become.

A typical day started about 8:30 a.m. I'd pack up my car with my files and documentation of the doctors I would be calling on. In 1990, we did not have personal computers yet, so everything we did was with paper. My territory was on the east side of Las Vegas, and I lived on the west side closer to Red Rock Canyon, a gorgeous national conservation area known for its hiking and biking trails and a popular tourist destination with a one-way thirteen-mile loop.

I drove my company car across the Las Vegas Strip on Tropicana Avenue past all the towering casinos. Usually, I could park at one office building and spend the day going from office to office. I took the stairs in six-story buildings to help myself stay in shape. Being physically fit was a big part of my life.

One tremendously sad story happened when a co-worker died by suicide. While I was in Texas, she had left me a voice mail saying, "Amy, this is Marilyn, and I want to be the first to welcome you to our team in Las Vegas. Looking forward to working with you. We have a lot in common, both being athletes. It's going to be fun!"

A week later, Marilyn was gone. I never met her in person, but within two months, I had begun to feel like I knew her. Every office in town loved Marilyn. Each time I walked in, they would tell me, "You remind me so much of Marilyn. We miss her." She was a college track star from Arizona State, and by all accounts, a fabulous and well-loved person. The strange thing was I seemed to go through a grieving process for a person I had never met. She left her powerful footprint on all the lives she touched. I am sorry I never had the chance to shake her hand.

In 1992, we received our first laptop computer, and we had training for an entire week in Los Angeles. One evening, we had a massive dinner on the beach, and it was beautiful and a little surreal to be treated so well.

While in L.A., the Olympic Committee happened to be hosting another Olympic Sports Festival, and I somehow found time to go watch the team handball games, and I ran into one of the longstanding handball coaches.

"What are you doing now, my dear?" Lazlo asked in his thick Hungarian accent.

"I'm working for Merck, a large pharmaceutical company," I replied proudly.

What he said next, I would never forget. "You are much too young to be all grown up. You will work for the rest of your life. You should play sports as long as you can."

I was deflated. I had been expecting approval and congratulations for landing a job with such a great company, but I soon found out others believed I should continue playing team handball for a few years.

In fact, when I ran into Peter, the man who was responsible for bringing team handball to the U.S. back in the early 1970s, he said, "When are you coming back to the Olympic Training Center?"

"I'm not coming back, Peter."

"Why not?"

"Because I have to make money and support myself."

"There will be plenty of time to make money."

I was not convinced. Mostly, I was frustrated that everyone I saw kept telling me I needed to keep playing while I could. In my mind, I was already twenty-five years old and had taken significant risks in becoming an Olympian the first time around. Why would I want to give up the opportunity to work for the country's number one company? Now I can see both sides of the argument, but back then, I only saw it as people not being supportive of me.

Driving back to the hotel that evening in Los Angeles traffic, I had quite a bit of time for reflection. At the end of the day, I am grateful for the decisions I made, even if it meant I had to grow up sooner than everyone else thought I should.

I credit my high level of computer skills to those early days and the continuous training I received over a course of eighteen years. A lot of people don't realize the value of training, but I consider it a great gift. Once I learned those skills, I took them anywhere I went.

I can't say it was a profession I ever saw myself being in, though I quickly realized how much I loved the academic challenges. Talking with physicians about how a drug works and the clinical data is a fascinating process, especially when discussing a new class of drugs. One of my products was Prilosec, and I had an awesome time teaching physicians about the mechanism of action—how it worked. It was the first drug of its kind.

I spent much of my time working with my customers and developing many friendships. One of my best friends was the late Tom Bolerjack, who was a Lt. Colonel in the Air Force. Tom was a pharmacist at Nellis Air Force Base. The first time I met him, I was new in my position, and he had a field day telling me everything I did wrong. Then he learned from his assistant that I had been in the Olympics and also had a pretty good game of racquetball. Being the competitive tough guy, he challenged me to a game. It wasn't about beating a girl—it was about beating a girl *Olympian*.

Tom invited me on base to join him and the guys for a friendly but highly competitive round robin of racquetball. When I beat him every single game, he walked out and had a whole new level of respect for me. After that day, we became great friends. Tom was a good man. I miss him.

My transition to working as a sales rep was a little bumpy at first. In my first week, I walked into a busy primary care office and confidently handed the receptionist my card. She took one look at it and tossed it back to me saying, "We don't use your products." I had to literally run out of the office because I was in tears. I got back to my car and sobbed. As an Olympian and Tennessee women's basketball player, people wanted my autograph. Now I was dealing with someone throwing my business card at me. I wondered, "Did I make the right decision?"

* * *

One of the best things about living in Las Vegas was having many family members and friends visit. Each year I lived there, Shelley, her husband Bob, and my nieces Ashley and Natalie would visit for two weeks.

I lived in a third-floor luxury apartment overlooking the pool area. The kids would swim every day, in spite of the blistering hot weather. One time they took a trip to Valley of the Fire State Park, located about sixty miles northeast of Las Vegas. It's well known for temperatures commonly reaching 120 degrees. They drove in my Jeep Wrangler with the top off. When they arrived back at my home, they were scorched like lobsters.

Living out west didn't keep me from having a close relationship with my family. We saw each other at least a few times a year and spoke regularly on the phone. The strong bond between Shelley, Bob, Ashley, and Natalie became paramount in later years.

The girls looked up to me, and I was affectionately known as "the fun aunt." They never wavered in their support of me when I went to war with my biggest competitor.

As many professionals say, it's not the mania that drives people to the doctor, it's the depression. After having a fairly long stretch of hypomania and normal periods, depression really hit me hard. It began to interfere with my ability to work, carry out daily activities, and engage in satisfying relationships. My illness was becoming more severe.

Shortly before having an extreme depressive episode, I moved from an apartment to a house with my roommate, Kandy. She worked for the military on a top-secret project for the Stealth fighter jet. Every Monday, she and a group of contractors flew out of Las Vegas to a secret place in the middle of the desert. She would not get back in town until late Thursday night, so I didn't see her often. We lived together but went our separate ways.

During the week, I did spend hours with my friend, Joel. He and I played racquetball six days a week. As soon as I was done with work, I would meet up with Joel, and we played for two to three hours. All of this worked out great until one day I walked into the racquetball court and found him looking extremely upset.

"Amy, I have something I need to tell you." He began to cry, which was unusual for him. He was an East Coast guy who stood only about 5'8" tall, but was tougher than nails.

"What is it, Joel? Is everything okay at home?"

"Yes." More sobs.

"You can tell me, it's okay." I leaned in, touching him on the shoulder.

Then he blurted it out. "I'm going to prison. Will you write to me?"

"Of course, I'll write to you. But what happened?"

I wasn't afraid or uncomfortable with what he was telling me. I was more disappointed I was going to be losing my friend for a while. With the way Joel was reacting, I honestly thought he was going to tell me he had a terminal illness.

I did not know much about Joel's background. I had met him in the racquetball court one day, and we became friends. I knew that in the past he was a professional gambler and had given it up when he met Shelby, his wife. But, apparently, while he was living in New Jersey, he was caught up in a gambling scheme. It took years to work its way through the court system, but he refused to testify against people, and because of that he was being sentenced to time in a federal prison.

There was no question I was going to miss him while he was gone, but this also meant that when I first began having symptoms of depression, no one was around to notice my behavior.

The depressive episode started with feeling more lethargic. It was as if my legs and arms were made of lead. I slept longer in the morning and did not get started with my day until almost noon. Because of the flexibility with my job, no one noticed. As long as I made my eight customer calls a day and kept up with my paperwork, I could get by, but it was a struggle.

One day, my friend Becky rang the doorbell. She had been calling, and I found myself not wanting to talk with anyone.

Amy Gamble

Being the persistent person she was, she showed up on my doorstep.

I heard her call my name. "Amy, are you there?"

I did not answer. After a while, she left. She never called again.

In my job as a sales representative, I called on doctors, so I knew several of them personally, but I decided to see a doctor who worked at the Olympic Training Center because I felt comfortable with him. He was a primary care doctor, so I went to see him not because I thought I had symptoms of depression, but because of all my physical symptoms like fatigue and lethargy. There was no part of me that believed I could have depression.

The doctor examined me and did several blood tests, and I will never forget when he came back into the room to tell me what he had found. He said very simply, "Amy, I think you have depression. I can prescribe a medication for you, and you'll get better."

I couldn't believe what he was saying. I told him, "I don't have depression. I don't have a mental illness. Not me."

He tried to reason with me but finally gave up. He told me if I changed my mind to come back and see him.

I never went back. That day began my intense repulsion of mental illness. I wanted no part of considering I might have depression, let alone any other mental illness. That was something my family members and other people had, not an Olympic athlete. There was no way I would embrace the idea that there was something wrong with me.

I ended up in a lengthy battle trying to go to work every day and carry on with my life. I don't remember exactly how long that episode lasted, but it wasn't severe enough for me to miss a significant amount of work. It did, however, interfere with my friendships because I isolated myself. I stopped almost all my exercises. I did the bare minimum to survive, and the rest of the time I slept. When Mom came to visit, she asked what she could do to help me get better. I persistently denied anything was wrong.

The only thing that really kept me going was a beautiful black Labrador named Chance. Some people would not think of going to a humane society to simply "look" at the dogs as a big deal, but I knew I could not leave without coming home with a dog.

On a hot, sunny day, I drove my red Jeep Wrangler with the top off to the humane society. I had always loved yellow Labradors since I saw the movie *Old Yeller*.

I could hear barks and yelps echoing throughout the building. I walked around, but after three times through the facility, I saw no yellow lab puppies. I was getting ready to leave when an old black lab caught my eye. I went over to her cage and stuck my hand through the fence to pet her. According to the paper outside her cage, she was eleven years old and over 100 pounds. I started to pet her, and suddenly the black lab in the adjacent cage began to bark and whine incessantly. I turned and said, "Okay. I'll pet you." But the feisty lab was making her presence known.

More shrill barking motivated me to quickly pay attention to her. I walked over and put my hand through the fence, touching her paw. She laid her head on my hand, as if to say, "Pick me. I'm the dog for you."

Her paperwork said she was ten months old and had only one day to live. One of the caretakers came and opened her cage for me. She ran past him right to me, knocking me on my butt. All I could do was pet her and give her my full attention.

Without much hesitation, I decided I wanted to adopt her. She was charcoal black with a beautiful, narrow face and attentive expression. I had no idea where I was going to keep her because I was living in an apartment and no dogs were allowed. I was moving into a house in two weeks, so I thought I could sneak her in my apartment until I moved.

Before I could take her home, she had to be spayed, so I hugged her and kissed her head goodbye. I went home feeling wonderful about finding my new best friend.

The day I went to pick Chance up, I was thrilled. She gave me her signature, yelping, high pitched bark. She would give me her official greeting for over sixteen years, outlasting all the human friends I met in the same time span. She was my wonder dog, my service dog, and my best, loyal friend. She was by my side if I was happy or if I was sad. While I was depressed, she stayed at my feet, and when I was manic, she ran beside me. If I had Chance today, she could wear a vest that service dogs wear for people with disabilities. She gave me a reason to get out of bed in the morning. Chance was one of the greatest gifts I ever had.

In spite of all my mental health challenges, in 1995 I managed to work my way into a promotion. I also had the opportunity to switch companies and go with a new start-up venture called AstraMerck. I was a high performer and a very effective salesperson. With the promotion came a move to Phoenix, Arizona and another life change that affected my mental well-being. I also had developed a relationship with one of my colleagues, Scarlett, who lived in Phoenix, and while many of these things were positive experiences, they were also very stressful.

* * *

As is true for many high achievers, I knew I had to continue to push myself for the next big challenge. Even though moving was a big adjustment, I also decided it was time to go back to school and earn a master's degree. Shortly after I moved, I had fallen into another depressive episode and gained weight from lack of exercise and eating too many carbohydrates. Some people with depression get carbohydrate cravings; I'm one of those people.

Life changes, major stressors, hormone problems, and underlying bipolar disorder made living feel like I was walking through three feet of mud wearing a pair of slippers. And, on top of all that, Mom continued to struggle with mania and psychosis. I was two thousand miles from West Virginia, so I wasn't directly affected on a daily basis, but I cared and worried about her.

On one occasion, Mom came to Arizona after my sister Shelley had called, frustrated with her that she was sick again and would not get help. I told Shelley I would buy Mom a plane ticket and she could stay with Scarlett and me for a while.

When Mom got to Phoenix, I knew the moment I picked her up at the airport that something was not quite right. She was having a severe manic episode that had escalated into psychosis.

I had rented a sports utility vehicle while she was in town for our sightseeing tours. My Jeep Wrangler was not the most comfortable ride. I thought if she came to Arizona, she might "snap out of it" and be all right. It really showed how little I understood bipolar disorder—and mental illness, for that matter.

We went to Jerome and Sedona, some of the most beautiful places on the planet, located about two hours from Phoenix. But she was floridly psychotic, which means she had lost touch with reality and the psychosis was very bad. At times, we could have a regular conversation, and other times she would be talking to someone who was not there. I felt scared and yet fascinated. I wanted to understand what she was going through, but she had no idea she was sick.

I remember asking, "Who are you talking to?

She said, "I am talking to Dr. Durick."

"Dr. Durick isn't in this car," I said with confusion.

Then she would get quiet and we'd drive for miles in silence. Honestly, I was much more comfortable with the silence than with her talking to someone who was not there.

After she had been with me for several days, she asked if she could take my car and go get a haircut. The closest salon was literally two minutes away, and I decided it might not be such a bad idea for her to get out of the house. She had been gone for over six hours, driving in a city she didn't know her way around, and she was overtly manic. I called the police and asked if they could find her. They tracked her to a gas station in Glendale, Arizona, lost. Scarlett and I drove to the gas station, and I brought her home.

Scarlett told me, "Aim, I like your mom, but she scares me. I'm sorry to say that, but that's how I feel." Even though I understood how Scarlett felt, she was my mother, and I was disappointed someone might be afraid of her.

A few days passed, and I called a local psychiatric hospital.

"My mother has bipolar disorder and she's psychotic. Do you have any beds available?"

"Does she have insurance?" the woman with the admissions department asked.

"Yes, she has insurance. Good insurance." I felt relieved when she said to bring her to the hospital.

I approached Mom and told her we needed to get her some help. She reluctantly got in the car with me, and we drove in total silence all the way to the hospital. I parked the car and took out her small travel case, and we walked into St. Joseph's Hospital in downtown Phoenix.

We got to the admissions desk, and Mom turned to me and emphatically said, "I am not going in this hospital!"

I grabbed her arm. "Yes, you are."

Before I could take another step, she pulled away and started running down the hall.

The nurse said, "She can't stay here. This is a voluntary hospital. If she doesn't want to be admitted, you can't make her."

"What am I supposed to do?" I asked, exasperated.

"Take her to a hospital emergency room where they accept involuntary commitments."

I raced down the hallway after Mom. She ran away from me and out the door. I finally caught up and pleaded with her until she got in the car.

While in the car, an argument ensued.

"I'm taking you to the hospital, and you're going to get treatment!"

"I didn't come all the way out here to Arizona to spend my time in a psychiatric hospital," she fired back.

"You either go into the hospital or go home," I yelled, along with a few expletives.

She looked at me like I was a big bad wolf trying to hurt her, when all I was trying to do was help.

"Get out of the car and walk, then." I didn't think she would take me up on it.

She got out of the car and started walking. I followed her.

"Mom, get back in the car. Please! I'm sorry I yelled at you."

She continued walking, and finally I convinced her to get back in. I drove the long way home, trying to find the other hospital, but I had no idea where it was. I eventually gave up.

When I got home, I picked up the phone and called Shelley. Shelley was my only sister who had not moved away. She and her husband Bob made their home in Glen Dale, about five miles from where we grew up. She and Bob had two kids, but were very close to our mother and father. Stress runs high in families who are dealing with mental health crisis situations, and ours was no exception. Often it resulted in heated discussions between siblings. This time was no different.

"I'm putting Esther on a plane and sending her home," I announced, using our mother's first name, as we sometimes did. "I think you need to pick her up at the airport and take her to the hospital."

"Do you think I don't know she needs to go to the hospital?" Shelley replied. She often felt like those of us siblings who lived away tried to tell her how to handle the situation.

"I understand you know what to do. Just pick her up, okay?" And I gave her the flight information.

I put her on a plane and sent her back home. Shelley picked her up at the airport and drove her to the hospital, where she ended up in inpatient psychiatric treatment. A few days later, my mother called my dad from the hospital for a ride home. He was there when my mother needed him, but he didn't really know how to handle the whole *mental illness thing*. Shelley had to step up and help out.

Some of these incidents might seem dramatic and traumatic, but many of us who live in the shadow of mental illness know high drama often comes with the territory. Now these events are simply part of my history, with only the scars left. Time does heal all wounds, and experience is our greatest teacher. What I have learned is I do whatever I have to do to survive in any given moment or circumstance, though some times have been easier than others.

Outside of my periodic depressive episodes, my life in Phoenix during this time was very rich. I had a few close friends, hiked frequently, and spent time making precious memories at an enchanting place called Apache Lake. Even the drive from Phoenix to the lake was magnificently touching. The winding dirt road through the hidden canyons brought me tremendous joy and served as a centering place for my spirit. Going to the lake almost every weekend for several years was a piece of heaven on earth. Scarlett loved to water ski, and Chance liked to ride the Polaris Jet Ski with me. Dealing with the high stress situations became so much easier because of all the healthy outlets I had.

Chapter 7

Getting Back in the Game

Sometimes being willing to take risks works for you, and other times, when you look back, you wonder what you were thinking. This was one of those crossroads in life where I can say the latter.

After the 1996 Olympics, a new women's professional basketball league was formed called the American Basketball League (ABL). There was a significant amount of hype and interest in women's basketball, and I was sitting on the sidelines thinking up ways I could try out for a professional team. It sounds a little far-fetched, given I had not played for seven years, but I wasn't the only person who was considering getting back into the game.

To follow through on this whim, I quit my successful career and moved to Philadelphia, where I helped the St. Joseph's women's basketball team with marketing in exchange for the opportunity to work out with the team. I was tied to St. Joe's through an old teammate and friend, Reg, from the University of Arizona, who was one of the assistant coaches.

Scarlett stayed behind in Phoenix with her Yorkie, Wiggley. We owned a home there, and was she working at a corporate office based out of Phoenix. Our home was a three-bedroom house with a pool which backed up to the Phoenix Mountain Preserve. We could walk out our door directly onto hiking trails. It was a great lifestyle. I was really apprehensive about leaving, and I knew I would miss Scarlett and my friends. But everyone around me was telling me it was an opportunity most people would never have, and I should take it.

I packed up my Jeep Wrangler and set off, with Chance sitting in the front seat for the entire ride across country. I remember stopping at a rest area outside of Columbus, and being so exhausted from driving all night long with no sleep, I climbed on top of a picnic table and lay down. Chance sat up and guarded me the entire time I slept. When I woke up, she would be sitting there, and when someone came close to me, she would let me know by growling and barking. I felt safe with Chance by my side.

But when I settled in Philadelphia, I slipped into a bad period of depression. Instead of being able to train, work out, and compete, I stayed in bed until noon, and then dragged myself to the office. I managed to play a little basketball, but never enough to bring up my skill level to the point of being able to compete. I was also finishing my master's degree, even in the midst of my struggles. After four months, I moved back to Phoenix.

Back in Arizona, my mood lifted a bit, and I began playing lots of basketball. Eventually, I got the opportunity to join the Seattle Reign as a replacement for a player who had been injured. One of my friends was the assistant coach of the team, and she asked me if I wanted to play.

There were five games left in the season. I played a few minutes in two games, and the rest of the time I sat watching from the bench. But I did manage to grab a rebound and get fouled in a game we played in Connecticut. I stepped up to the foul line with over 10,000 screaming fans yelling, "Miss it." The first shot was an air ball, not even close to the rim or backboard. I looked over at my teammates, and they were yelling encouragement. I made the next shot.

It was a cool experience, and I certainly went down in the record books, but it was not worth the sacrifices I had made in my career. And I don't know if having bipolar disorder made any difference in my decisions. It's one of those times when viewing it from the rearview mirror makes it clearer to see the mistakes. Staying with my secure corporate position would have been the wise decision.

* * *

Life in Phoenix was peaceful, filled with sunshine, which really helped with my depression, and I had lots of meaningful friendships. Scarlett and I maintained our relationship throughout the time I was living in Philadelphia, but I was jobless, and my one-thousand-dollar paycheck from the ABL didn't pay many bills. I couldn't jump-start my career in Arizona, so in 1997, Scarlett and I moved back to Philadelphia so I could work at AstraMerck again. It helped that she was promoted to another position that worked out of Philadelphia. She was successfully climbing the corporate ladder, which made it easier to relocate. We packed up the car, including Chance and Wiggley, and headed back east.

Until we could buy a house in Philadelphia, the dogs went on retreat in West Virginia and stayed with my parents. Chance had spent several months with my mom and dad while I was in Philadelphia the first time around. Daddy had gotten very accustomed to driving in his truck with Chance riding shotgun. He would drive up to the local country grocery store, Butch's Corner, and all the guys he hung out with in the morning would always comment about Chance waiting in the driver's seat. In the meantime, Wiggley would make his way on my dad's lap while he sat in a blue La-Z-Boy chair in front of the fireplace.

For me, personally, three moves in just over one and half years, and two months spent in Seattle, was a little over the top. This would stress out anybody, with or without a mental illness. It took a toll on my mental health, and my physical health was not far behind.

It wasn't until many years later that I was diagnosed with polycystic ovarian syndrome, but I spent countless hours in the emergency room with ruptured cysts and severe endometriosis. Once I was living in Philadelphia, the gynecologist suggested I take a treatment regimen of a three-month injection that would put my body into early menopause.

What the doctor failed to mention was that the drug Lupron had a warning for psychiatric disturbances. In fact, people who have an underlying mental health condition are more at risk for developing additional psychiatric problems. The only diagnosis I officially had at this juncture was depression. I'm not sure if I would have even considered telling her I had a family history of mental illness, but it would have been nice to have been given the option of knowing. The hormonal challenges I had was also a risk factor for depression, and I was well on my way to a cataclysmic explosion.

Chapter 8

The Bipolar Express

Going back to work proved a very successful endeavor. Thanks to my drive to excel, within a year, I was promoted to a director and given the opportunity to design my own department. I hired six people, helped transition my team through a merger, and was doing quite well—until a manic episode changed my life forever and impacted many people around me.

It began after I had presented at a national meeting in New Orleans. I took a side trip with Scarlett to Key West. I had so much energy there, I could not sit still. While Scarlett rested, I rollerbladed around the town so many times that I was sunburned by the end of the day and had difficulty sleeping at night. The mania engine had begun to roar.

After our vacation, I returned to Philadelphia and went back to work. A side effect of Lupron caused hot flashes that kept me awake at night. I was also maintaining a social schedule that would've been nearly impossible to keep up with in my most healthy moments. I spent a great deal of time hanging out with Reg. Her Irish heritage encouraged going out and having a few drinks. Many times after work, I went home and took care of the dogs then headed out to meet up with Reg and other friends from St. Joe's. I often stayed out until 1:00 a.m. and then got up at 6:00 a.m. to get ready for work. Scarlett wasn't home very often because she was traveling across the country for work, and she was also working on an Executive Master's in Business on the west coast. For the most part, it was just me, the dogs, lots of friends, and my family who visited because Philadelphia was only a six-hour drive from where I grew up.

The bipolar train was rolling, and it was moving faster and faster. My thoughts would jump from one subject to the next. I had all these grandiose ideas, beyond my usual idea-oriented self. People were raising their eyebrows, but it wasn't bad enough to make anyone think something was wrong.

Connie, who was my boss at the time, said to me very sternly, "Stop telling people you can create workshops when you don't have the expertise to do it."

I have since learned a symptom of mania is grandiose thoughts in which a person believes she can do many things, even if it is not realistic.

* * *

One morning, I had horrible stomach pain.

"Julie, I can't bear this pain in my stomach," I said to my friend while we were having breakfast at a local restaurant. "Please take me to the hospital."

"What's wrong with you?" she asked, not so convinced I wasn't joking.

"I don't know. I just can't stand this anymore."

Finally, Julie agreed to take me. I was admitted because of the abdominal pain.

My doctor gave me injections of a potent pain medication, but after three days in the hospital and multiple injections, a nurse said, "I'm not giving you any more of this drug. It's making you crazy."

To make matters worse, I never even had a physical diagnosis. It was probably a ruptured cyst or two, but I'll never know.

I started crying uncontrollably. I was having paranoid thoughts, and I believed everyone was out to get me. Anyone who came to visit me was the good guy or the bad guy, an angel or a devil. I had lost insight into my condition, and was in the midst of a psychotic episode, the first of my life.

I called and asked Shelley to come to the hospital, and she flew in to be with me, even though she was busy with her own family. My niece Natalie was in college, and Ashley was a junior in high school, so the kids did not need continuous care. I didn't ask my mother to come because she was having her own struggles with bipolar disorder.

Shelley and Scarlett tried to tell the doctor something was wrong with me, but the doctor was anxious to leave the hospital that day, mentioning she needed to go to her daughter's basketball game. She did not help me, and the situation escalated. I was in a mental health crisis in a hospital, and they did nothing to avert the situation. If I'd had a physical illness, this would have been a malpractice lawsuit waiting to happen.

I woke up suddenly one night feeling like a surge of electricity was shooting through my veins. I got out of bed quietly so I didn't wake Scarlett, who was sleeping in a chair. I wandered down the hallway to the chapel, yelling at the top of my lungs and gathering the notice of several people. Not in my right mind, I grabbed a framed picture off the wall and slammed it onto the floor. I thought God commanded me to do it.

I dropped to my knees and began rolling around in the glass. I finally got the attention of Scarlett and a doctor, who called security. The guard took me back to my room, securing me to my bed. While I can remember what happened, at the time I did not know what I was doing. When the brain malfunctions, the delusions seem incredibly real. In my mind, God was really talking to me, telling me people were evil, and to get their attention I needed to make a big scene.

I don't know why my delusions were grandiose religious ones, meaning I thought I was directly talking to God, and he commanded me to do something such as make a scene and break the picture frame. It felt real. Of course, I can look back and know I was not in my right mind, but in the moment, I did not know I was ill. Psychosis is very cruel.

One of the problems I had after I recovered was learning to pray again. It brought up memories of my psychosis, and that was a painful memory I wanted to quickly forget. It was the first time I would struggle with those feelings, but it would not be the last.

I was restrained more than fourteen hours before a psychiatrist was called in for a consultation. The restraints were something called "four point." My arms and legs were bound by leather restraints to the frame of the bed. I could not move. Most of the night and well into the morning, I slept, because they had given me a potent injection called Haldol. The next day, I was transported to a psychiatric facility.

When I got into the ambulance, it was the first time I had ever been transported by emergency medical technicians. They let me sit up on the bed and did not restrain me. We rode in silence to the psychiatric hospital. I felt as if I had done something wrong, but my mind was not clear enough to understand exactly what that something was. It all felt more like punishment than being cared for. But I suppose that's what the trauma of being restrained for fourteen hours will do.

It is often misunderstood that during psychosis a person does not have the capacity to feel, and she won't remember what happened. Yet I not only felt pure terror, I also remember that during the episode, all I could think of was the 1970's movie, *One Flew Over the Cuckoo's Nest* and Jack Nicholson's character having a lobotomy. I wondered if this was going to happen to me.

The first thing I noticed about the psych unit in Philadelphia was that I couldn't get out. The door was locked. I knew the units were locked for the safety of patients and others. The whole idea of inpatient care is to stabilize the patients and get them on their way so they can be treated on an outpatient basis. But I didn't know I wasn't well. I don't like to use the term "lost my mind" because it simplifies all the complexities of what's going on, and it perpetuates the stigma of mental illness. I was not crazy, but I had an untreated mental illness and was in the midst of a psychotic episode.

I only stayed in the psychiatric hospital for a little over a day, and then my family took me to Johns Hopkins Mood

Disorders Center in Baltimore. The doctors there quickly diagnosed me with bipolar disorder. Because I had family members with the illness, it put me at a greater risk of developing it. It didn't mean I would have bipolar disorder, but it made a differential diagnosis much easier when they found out my family history and the symptoms I was experiencing.

I didn't believe it.

At the time, I was firmly convinced the Lupron I was taking had caused my psychotic episode. I was in fierce denial that I had a mental illness, but in my defense, no one explained to me what was happening.

When I woke up after my first night at Johns Hopkins, my eyes were closed so tightly a tear couldn't squeeze out. It took every ounce of courage I had to open them. At first, I thought I had died and gone to hell. Turning slowly to my right, I saw a woman pushing an IV cart, her bones protruding like a skeleton with skin. Sitting in deafening silence, I returned to staring straight ahead. I was in a fog of confusion trying to sort out where I was and exactly how I had gotten there, but with little success.

In reality, I was in a large inpatient psychiatric treatment facility on a floor for patients with mood and eating disorders. I later learned that eating disorders have the highest mortality rate of all mental illnesses. I had lost a friend to anorexia. She and I had played several games of racquetball together. In the middle of the summer, she would show up to play in multiple layers of sweats, in hopes of dropping a few pounds by sweating weight off, as if she were a boxer trying to make weight for a bout. Somehow, being hospitalized with people who were struggling gave me a sense of greater compassion for those with this life-threatening illness.

There was a young girl about fifteen years old whose mother told me she was diagnosed with bulimia. She was a basketball player, and I told her mother I played college and professional basketball. I had a pair of shorts with the team logo from my days playing professional basketball, and I asked her mother if she minded if I gave them to her daughter. It was a small gesture, but I hoped it would help her feel better, if only for a moment or two.

They gave me a private room, which was great except it was right next to a guy who had a domestic violence charge. I could hear his attorney in the room talking about what he should say in court. I lay in my bed shaking with terror. I was afraid he was going to hurt me. Not to mention the fact I shared a private bathroom with him, which really weirded me out.

One evening, after falling asleep trembling, a nurse who had short, blonde hair and stood about 5'10" leaned over my bed. "I brought you your medications. Do you want to sit up and take them?" I shook my head. She noticed I was shaking. "You poor thing, you're having withdrawal symptoms." She left the room and returned with an injectable detox medication. "This is going to help you."

"Withdrawal from what?"

"You had narcotics in your blood."

"Any narcotics I have in my system came from inpatient hospitalization. I've never done illegal drugs."

I didn't want the injection, but I was miserable. Shaking, sweating, trembling, and terrified out of my mind, I was trying to recover from a manic and psychotic episode, while dealing with all the drugs in my system, and they were all put there by healthcare professionals. What the heck kind of treatment was I getting?

A couple of times a day, the nurses would come in and give me an injection and a handful of pills. I decided since they were monitoring my blood levels I had better take the medication or I would never be released.

I attended a group therapy a few days after I was admitted. A young man about twenty years old was preparing to have electroconvulsive therapy, commonly known as shock therapy. ECT has been shown to be highly effective for people who have treatment resistant severe depression. Some even use it for those who have bipolar disorder.

One of the male nurses told me, "ECT is good treatment. You're gonna need it one day."

I looked at him like he was from Mars. I had to hold my tongue because there was no way anyone was ever going to put electrodes on my head and cause medically induced seizures. But I was terrified they were going to take me in some back room and do something to me. The delusions had not completely gone away, and the way some people talked to me made the situation worse.

After six days in the hospital, I was released. I was given a handful of prescriptions and no patient education information. In no way was I ready to be discharged. My fear of never getting out was far from the more likely reality of not staying in long enough. In the United States, the average inpatient psychiatric stay is seven days.

I have learned even the best treatment facilities can and do make mistakes when it comes to those with mental illness, especially when family members are not given the opportunity to provide feedback about someone's behavior. Often, it's the family members who can judge a person's normal state of mind. Somewhere there should be a balance between respecting those of us who have a mental illness and having flexibility in the laws that protect us in our most vulnerable moments.

Chapter 9

The Bipolar Dam Breaks

After leaving the hospital that day, I had no intention of seeing the doctor they'd suggested. Instead, all I felt was an extreme sense of paranoia. I was not thinking clearly, and I could not yet decipher what was real and what was delusions. Simply put, I was not stable.

I can't remember exactly how long I had been out of the hospital, but it was less than a couple of weeks. I answered the phone one very early morning, and it was Scarlett's parents letting us know her grandfather had passed away. I spent the rest of the day arranging for someone to take care of the dogs, while also making flight reservations to Houston, Texas.

On the way to Houston, we had a change of planes in the Pittsburgh airport. I had gotten very agitated on the plane.

"I'm getting off in Pittsburgh!" I told Scarlett firmly.

"No, Aim. You're not," she replied, still in a state of shock from getting the news her grandfather had passed away and dealing with my recent high drama mental health crisis.

"Yes, I am. Get away from me!" I shouted at her in the middle of the airport.

I waved down a guy driving one of the transport golf carts, and he took me to the baggage claim area. I walked outside the door and called my mother to come pick me up. The Pittsburgh airport was only an hour from my hometown.

Within two weeks after being released from the hospital, I would be back in another hospital in my hometown. I went from hospital emergency room to emergency room having panic attacks. I also had bronchitis and asthma, so the rapid heart rate, sweating, tightening chest, and shortness of breath from a panic attack made my underlying symptoms even worse.

Finally, during a severe panic attack, my parents called 911. The ambulance came and took me to one of the local hospitals. While I waited in my bed in the ER, a nun came in my room to talk with me.

"How are you feeling?"

"How am I feeling? I feel horrible. I would be better off dead."

She turned around and bolted for the door. A few moments later a doctor came in my room.

"I need for you to sign these papers for voluntary commitment to the psych ward."

"No, thank you."

"If you don't sign, we'll have you committed involuntarily. It's really better for you if you sign yourself in. Think about it. You'll be able to sign yourself out too."

He made it sound like I had choices in the matter, and I liked the idea of having some say of when I would leave. I signed the papers.

My mother had told the ER doctors I had bipolar disorder, but no attempt was made to obtain my medical records. I was placed on an entirely different medication regimen and told I had anxiety.

In the psych ward, I finally opened my eyes one by one and found myself in the ugliest place imaginable. The walls were peeling, pale colored paint, and the room smelled of antiseptics. I turned my head slowly to the left and looked up and saw a camera in the corner staring back at me. I was so afraid to move, for fear someone would hurt me more than I had already been hurt. The emotional pain I felt was much more intense than any physical pain I had experienced with any of my athletic injuries.

"Dear God," I prayed silently, "please help me understand why I am here in this awful place." My head swam with information, trying to recall how I had ended up lying in the bed.

I heard voices outside my room, although I could not understand what they were talking about. I assumed they must be talking about me, at least part of the conversation. I turned my head to the right and noticed a metal tray with a pitcher of water and a cup. I slid out of bed and made my way to the attached bathroom. I tried to turn the handle, but the door was locked. I got back in bed and asked myself, "Why are you here?"

At one point, the treating physician looked at me and said, "If you have bipolar disorder, you are the strangest bipolar patient I have ever seen." How's that for confidence in the diagnosis?

* * *

The only pleasant thing about that hospital stay was playing dominos with a young man, probably in his twenties. I was barely able to lift my head because I had been given a horse's dose of psychotropic medications. But I kept my head in a tilted position where I could play the game. If I were looking down viewing the person I had temporarily become, tears would come to my eyes. Knowing how the future would unfold strikes a deep emotion inside of me, and in a split moment of reflection, I wish the first opportunity for me to be given mental health treatment had been handled differently. Now that I know so much more about bipolar disorder and psychosis, it would have helped me to have been given a full explanation of how this illness works. I would have liked to have heard, "Amy, bipolar disorder will destroy your life if you don't find the proper treatment regimen."

Unfortunately, we cannot change the past.

It was at this juncture I truly had the opportunity to change the trajectory of my life. I could have saved myself and others from so much pain and suffering as a result of my untreated bipolar disorder, but I felt safe in my denial. I didn't like how people looked at me when they found out I was diagnosed with bipolar disorder. I was once respected and adored, and now I felt like people didn't want to have anything to do with me. Of course, my family and closest friends were trying their best to understand. But stigma—shame, blame, discrimination, misunderstanding—were all at play.

Some of my feelings about how people treated me were real and some weren't because I was paranoid about having been admitted to a psychiatric hospital. I felt insecure. I felt like everyone knew, and in some cases I felt the need to tell them if they didn't know. The bipolar dam had broken, and my life would never be the same.

It also didn't help that I didn't have consistent care. I had seen a total of five different physicians, and they all had various explanations for what had happened. They made it so much more confusing. And then someone told me I did not have bipolar disorder, and that was music to my ears. I didn't want to listen to any other reasonable explanation. It was all going to have to play itself out, and the outcome would not be positive.

A few years later I found a notebook full of documentation of my hospital stays. I had taken all the information to an attorney in Philadelphia. I felt like I was completely mistreated and there was a ton of truth in that. At the end of those fifteen total days in the hospital, starting with the community based hospital for stomach pain, I was given twenty-five different oral medications and forty injections. My hips were bruised and the nerves were damaged. It would take over a year to heal the physical aspects, and more than ten years to heal the mental wounds. The attorney told me I didn't have a case. Perhaps I didn't. But at the very least, it would have been nice to have an apology.

Following Mom's lead, I took a three-month leave of absence after being released from the hospital before I returned to work. Scarlett had been promoted, and the new position was located back in Phoenix. I had considered staying by myself in Philadelphia, but felt like it was not the best place for me, so I took a lateral move with my company and returned to Phoenix.

I remember having a conversation with one of my mentors who helped me obtain a National Account Director position that could be worked from Phoenix, even though it would mean I would have to travel to different parts of the country.

He said, "You are talented enough to do any number of jobs. What do you want to do?"

I felt relieved when he told me this, but somewhat confused because he knew what I had been through. I expected all people to treat me differently, mostly because of my own embarrassment. What I discovered was there were many more people who were compassionate and understanding than I first thought, perhaps because they didn't know the whole story. To me, the whole story made me feel "crazy." I was my own worst critic, consumed with self-stigma and a real live victim of the healthcare system.

I stopped taking any medications because I stubbornly refused to acknowledge I had a mental health condition. I resolved what had happened to me was a medication side effect, and I told anyone who would listen my trials and tribulations with the healthcare system. I even wrote a letter to First Lady Hillary Clinton telling her about the healthcare system and its need for changes. I don't know why unstable people with mental illness reach out to the government, but it seems that many of them do, myself included.

Returning to Phoenix did help me return to better health, but any chance I had to focus on myself was averted. I needed all my strength and energy to help support my family, who were dealing with yet another crisis. My father had been diagnosed with brain cancer.

Chapter 10

My Father's Passing

When someone receives a diagnosis of a glioblastoma brain tumor, you hope for an extension of his or her life, as it's the best possible outcome. My father had two surgeries to remove the mass, but it's an extremely aggressive tumor and grows back rapidly.

As my dad's health progressively got worse, so did his functioning. Eventually, he ended up bedridden. Mom quit her job to take care of him, and Cindy temporarily moved to West Virginia to help. Shelley was always a mainstay who helped take care of everyone. It was expected that I would do my part as well.

Growing up, I was known as "Daddy's girl." I loved many of the things he was interested in. He taught me how to hunt, fish, and shoot a basketball. I can still see him sitting in the back yard, and me begging him to throw a softball with me from the time I was eight years old.

"Daddy, please throw with me!"

"All right, go get the gloves." He would tease me when I missed a ball, saying, "Come on, butterfingers," in a playful way, but always motivating me to do better. He would say, "Keep your eye on the ball." His coaching and attention he paid to me would help me become an All-Star softball player and ultimately an Olympian.

All my sisters were very athletic. The twins, Shelley and Sherry, were almost nine years older than I was. Bonnie and Cindy were five and six years older. All of us were involved in 4-H. Everyone except Sherry raised a cow and learned the hard work that comes with taking care of animals. My dad would come home from work, we would have dinner, and then he would say, "Time to go to the barn. Get your shoes on."

My Aunt Mary Francis and Uncle Forest owned a forty-acre farm adjacent to our property. I could walk to their house in five minutes. They were more like grandparents to us all. The barn where the cattle were kept was a part of their farm, so when we went to feed the cows, we often stopped in to visit.

I loved the hard work of cleaning a cow pen and working in the hayfield. I imagine I developed the baseline of my strength by lifting haybales. The summer was always a time for two things—allergies and baling hay. It was a guarantee.

My mother would say, "I don't know why you want to go in the hot, damn dirty hayfield."

I would tell her, "I like to help," and then I would run out the door to find my father. If everything went right for me, Daddy would let me drive the big, red Farmall tractor. I believe that was my real underlying motivation. I loved to drive the tractor.

When I was nine years old, Daddy taught me how to drive the tractor. Prior to that, I sat on his lap and he would let me steer the wheel. But when I could reach the pedals, it was time for me to drive by myself. He had an old-fashioned plow he used to mark the rows in the garden. The plow was attached to the back of the tractor, and he would hold down on it as the metal shovel turned the soil, which is called marking a row. I spent significant time with my dad outside doing farm work, and I loved almost every minute of it.

Another motivation for being in the hayfield was hanging out with my best friend Alex. He had sun-bleached blond hair and was so thin he would have blown away in the wind.

He liked to ride his bike, play board games, and create games like "mail man" and "salesman." In the basement of my house, we played together for hours, learning how to be good sports even when we lost at the game of the day.

During the summer months, Alex's father Roland baled hay with my dad. Alex did his best to move a haybale toward the wagon. He wasn't quite strong enough to lift the bale, but he tried really hard.

Occasionally, my dad would ride Alex and me out to Roth's Store, a local mom and pop shop that sold soda and candy. Once we made it to Roth's, Alex would choose a chocolate drink called Yoo-hoo. I would get an orange soda. Both of us would sit in the back of my dad's pickup truck and let our hair blow freely in the wind.

One summer, Alex became very ill. We were both at the fairground for the annual 4-H cattle show and sale. I remember playing on all the tractors on exhibit, one of our favorite pastimes. But shortly after the fair ended, Alex was admitted to the hospital.

He stayed in the hospital for more than a week and never made it home again. They said he had appendicitis, but I never really knew how or why he had to die. I only recall visiting him in the hospital and buying him a get-well card with a cow on the front.

One morning my mom came in my room and said, "Alex Caldwell died today." He was twelve years old. I started to cry. I buried my head in the pillows and mourned for my best friend who had his life taken away many years too soon.

Every time I walk in the woods I take a minute and think about Alex. I can't help but wonder if he had lived, if would we still be friends. In my heart, I know there's no way to replace the memories we made. He will always be remembered.

* * *

I really had the best of both worlds growing up. My father taught me all the things about the outdoors and sports that I came to love. My mother made sure I had nine years of piano lessons and went to the symphony. I developed a vast view of what was possible by having exposure to so many different things and interesting people.

On one hot summer day in Arizona, I had returned home from a long hike with Chance. Wiggley had died a few months prior from kidney disease. The phone rang, and it was Cindy. She said my father didn't have much longer to live, and I needed to come home and stop worrying about my career. "You only get one father," she said.

It wasn't that I didn't want to help, but I was experiencing a huge amount of stress from the numerous trips I was making to visit my father and family. I was also working full-time and traveling with my job—and I was not taking my medication for bipolar disorder. Against my better judgment, I agreed to take the time off work, and I went home to stay with my parents in West Virginia.

When I arrived at my parents' home, the first thing I noticed was the hayfield had not been cut. I trudged through the four-feet-tall grass and found my way to the barn. The old door creaked as I opened it, in dire need of some grease. I saw the red Farmall parked in its usual place. I climbed on the tractor and pulled the metal starter. The 1950s tractor had seen better days.

I walked down to my Aunt Mary Francis's home. She was happy to see me.

"I wish someone would cut this field behind my house so I can see the deer. It's too high. Your dad always cut it, but he's not able."

"I'll cut it," I said eagerly. "But we need a new tractor."

"Well," she said intently, "sounds like a good idea. But we have to talk to Shelley. She's my money lady."

Shelley liked the idea. Mary Francis handed us her checkbook and told us to get whatever tractor we wanted.

We drove about forty-five minutes across the Ohio River into Ohio and went to a John Deere tractor dealership. I don't believe those guys had ever had two women walk into their store and say, "We're here to buy a tractor!" I doubt very seriously it has ever happened again at this particular store. Maybe somewhere else in the United States, but not in a small town in Ohio.

I test drove a couple different models and tried out the brush hog. Shelley wrote the check, and we had the first new green tractor ever delivered to the farm.

I had a tutorial on how to use the hydraulics, engage the power train, and a few other pertinent things one needs to know to drive a tractor. I immediately began cutting the hayfield, and it took me several days to finish the entire farm. Then I walked into Daddy's bedroom and said, "I cut it all."

His blue eyes followed me around the room, but he could not speak. I always imagined he would have said, "Damn, why did everyone wait until I was dying to buy a new tractor?"

Three weeks later, my father passed away at home, and I learned watching the death of a loved one can be deeply traumatic. I saw my father take his last breath, and I closed his eyes after he died. This time had been so stressful, I felt like my head was going to explode. That stress, along with sleepless nights and too much self-medicating with alcohol, proved too much, and I had a manic episode the day of the funeral.

We had many relatives and friends from out of town who came to the funeral home. The service was at the Lutheran church I had grown up attending. Sitting in those pews reminded me of all the time I spent as a worship assistant, from the time I was fifteen until I left for college. Sundays meant two things to me—go to church, and go to the YMCA to play basketball with the guys. My mother would say, "If you don't go to church, you don't go anywhere else." It was a mandatory thing, but I didn't mind because for the most part I really enjoyed it.

The funeral service consisted of a few speakers talking about my father's life. I was one of the speakers, even though I had already begun to have a manic episode. My mind was racing and I was losing touch with reality. Emotions were running high, and my family members were noticing something was wrong with me.

Instead of sticking to the script and having a peaceful gathering at our home, I decided we would invite everyone to my dad's favorite place, a hunting cabin we referred to as the "shack," located about a mile into the woods. I filled coolers with an overabundance of beer and soda. My sisters and mother were fuming.

But people came to the shack in droves. We sat around in a big circle from evening until late at night, and everyone told their favorite story about my father. I wanted it to be a celebration of his life. And in my euphoric mania stage, it was time for a party.

The next day I took Scarlett back to the airport. I was staying behind for a reason clouded by my manic episode. After I dropped her off, I rented a yellow Mustang convertible. When I parked the car in the driveway, Cindy came roaring out of the house.

"You're *crazy*! Do you think this is a party? My dad just died, and you're running around like this is a time to have fun. You're sick! Get out of here!" She was screaming at the top of her lungs.

I went into the house and packed my bags.

I don't remember what she said, but she screamed the entire time I was in the house and followed me all the way back to the car. She had a yellow lab who got on the floor of my car when I opened the door. Even Bell wanted to get away from her. She was calling me crazy, but in fact, she had come unhinged.

I started driving on Interstate 70 west toward Columbus, Ohio with the intention of getting to the airport and flying back to Arizona. Mentally, I was grappling between reality and the start of delusions, and I began to think people were trying to hurt my Aunt Mary Francis. I turned around before I got to the airport and began driving east. I drove an hour and then turned around again and headed back to Columbus. By this time, it was late at night and my head was bobbing. I was jerking to stay awake.

I stopped at a hotel in the early morning hours, but the lady told me they were full. I continued to drive back to West Virginia.

I had learned my dad's cousin Neva was in the hospital, and I decided at 5:00 a.m. to go visit her. True to form, I visited the hospital chapel first. I began to think I was an angel on a mission from God to save the good people.

I found Neva's room and sat in a chair until she woke up.

Startled, she said, "Amy, what are you doing here?"

"I came to visit you," I replied, very cheery for the early morning hours.

"Go home to your mother. You go home now," she commanded.

I wished her well and headed to my mother's house. When I got there, the door was locked, so I started pounding on it. I scared her, but when she realized it was me, she started yelling. In fairness to everyone involved, I think emotions were raw, and bipolar was rearing its ugly head at a very inconvenient time.

Scared by her temperament, I got in the car and sped down the road to Aunt Mary Francis's house. I was convinced my uncle and sister were trying to hurt her. I barged in the door and yelled, "Don't worry, Mary Francis. I'll save you!"

They called the police.

My family had me committed to a psychiatric hospital under the state's mental health hygiene involuntary commitment order.

During the three weeks I stayed with my parents, I had a very difficult time sleeping. At one point, I called a primary care doctor, but he would not see me. I never thought of going to an urgent care to get treatment for no sleep. I also did not realize how dangerous it was for me to go days with only sleeping a few hours at a time. I have since learned that my number one trigger for a bipolar episode is either sleeping too much or too little.

An involuntary commitment is when someone fills out specific paperwork through the court system declaring you are a danger to yourself or others. Once the paperwork is submitted, the sheriff's department or paramedics are sent to pick up the person who is having a mental health crisis. If the police show up, people are then handcuffed and placed into the back of a police cruiser and either taken to a brief hearing or taken directly to a psychiatric treatment facility.

When the deputy sheriff rolled up in front of my parents' home, I knew they were there for me. They walked me down the sidewalk with one of the deputy sheriffs mumbling about how he knew my sisters. He was shaking his head, as if trying to shake off the fact I was having a psychotic episode.

We got to the car, and he turned to his partner and said, "We aren't going to do this handcuff thing. She's cooperating. Just let her sit in the back seat without the cuffs."

I remember thinking, "Handcuffs? What have I done wrong?" Even in my confused state of mind, I knew handcuffs would not be pleasant.

I got in the back seat of the sheriff's car, with my mind racing, and I said, "Are you guys the good guys or the bad guys?"

One of them replied, "We're the good guys, Amy." And they both laughed. It was a good thing they had a sense of humor, because I was with them for the entire day before I finally got taken to the hospital.

I wish there was a better way to treat people who are having a mental health crisis. It's very traumatic whenever the police are involved, not only for the person who is experiencing the crisis, but also the loved ones who are applying for the order. But the truth was, I needed help, and they tried to get help for me. Unfortunately, it all backfired.

Less than thirty-six hours after being hospitalized, I was released. I wasn't released because my mental health miraculously improved, but because of the way the hospital was interpreting an involuntary commitment law. After being held against my will for a short time, the facility where I was said they would have to transfer me back to my place of residence in Arizona since I was from another state and most likely told them I wanted to go home.

West Virginia state law says an individual has the right to request a hearing be held in a county of his or her choice. At the time, I was psychotic, I did not understand I needed treatment, and I was not capable of deciding whether I should be released from the hospital. All I remember was confusion and a lot of discussion among the doctor and hospital personnel. I got one prescription for medication, and I was sent on my way. I don't know whether they interpreted the law correctly, but nonetheless, they released me under the pretense of not being a "danger to myself or others." My family didn't even know they let me go.

Once released, I called a taxi. The driver picked me up and said, "Where are you headed today?"

"I want to buy a new car!"

"Do you know what car dealership you want to buy your car from?"

"No. Take me where you would go."

He looked in the rearview mirror and said, "Are you Amy Gamble, the basketball player?"

"Yes, I am. Are you an angel?"

He dropped me off in front of the dealership, and I drove away with a new car. Not because I needed one, but because whatever was going on in my mind said I should have one. Needless to say, my purchase was not well received by anyone.

After several days, I checked myself out of the hotel I had moved to after my father died and set out on the road back to Arizona. There was something about the sound of the wheels' monotonous grinding over the roadway that soothed my anxiety. I have heard of parents taking their babies for a ride in the car to help them go to sleep. It has a calming effect. Even now I do some of my best creative thinking when I am on the highway driving.

Fortunately, I continued to take the medication I had been prescribed. It was an anti-psychotic and highly effective. By the time I got to Knoxville, Tennessee, I was relatively "normal," and only a bit manic. I contacted an old teammate, Mary O., who was living in Knoxville, and she invited me to a kayaking outing. We spent the day together talking about old times and making some good memories.

Meanwhile, my family had no idea where I was. I had taken my cell phone battery out so no one could contact me. They knew I was upset about the hospitalization, but they were worried about where I was headed.

While in Knoxville, I contacted my former coach Pat Summitt, who was still coaching at the University of Tennessee. She invited me to lunch. I had last seen Coach Summitt in 2000, the prior year, at an event I was involved in called the AstraZeneca Hoops for the Cure. When I saw her this time, she gave me a tour of her office and had someone show me the locker room, and then invited me to her home. I met her son, Tyler, who was about twelve years old. The next day she and I had lunch together, and she wished me well when I left.

I was packing up my things in Knoxville, getting ready to head back to Arizona, when Coach Summitt called and asked if I was headed to Atlanta. She wanted me to follow her son and his nanny through Atlanta to a soccer tournament. She was unable to go because she was announcing a WNBA game on ESPN. She thought if I was traveling that way, she would feel more comfortable with her son and nanny traveling through Atlanta with another person.

I agreed and had a wonderful couple of days with them. We spent most of our time watching Tyler play soccer. In the morning, he and a friend would knock on my door and I would go to breakfast with the boys. We chatted about anything that interested them. A couple of times we went to the racquetball court and played. Growing up babysitting the neighbors' kids helped me to develop a gift for talking and relating to young people. It is still one of the qualities I like best about myself.

* * *

I have told this story for a number of reasons.

First, to really demonstrate that having a mental illness does not always mean you are "crazy." Unless a person is in a mental health crisis, which generally means he or she is either suicidal or psychotic, it is very difficult to discern when a person may be experiencing symptoms. Thankfully, I was taking medication and it began working rather rapidly. I was not one hundred percent well, but I was not delusional either.

Second, it's important for me to demonstrate how many people made an impact in my life. In the times when I needed people to be kind to me, my connections from Tennessee really stepped up in a big way. Pat Summitt always said, "Once a Lady Vol, always a Lady Vol," and she was true to her word. I will be forever grateful.

Chapter 11

Losing What You Need Most

Getting back home safely to Arizona—in my new car—was a blessing. Scarlett, Chance, and the yellow lab we had rescued, Goldie, were at home to greet me. Scarlett had been really worried about me, but unsure how to help.

One of the first things I did was find a psychiatrist and schedule an appointment. My search was limited to those who were covered by my insurance plan, so by the time I found a doctor, it was another two months before I could get an appointment. In the meantime, I'd run out of the medication prescribed by the physician in West Virginia.

In the interim, I did see a nurse practitioner who prescribed an anti-depressant for me. I didn't know as much about bipolar disorder as I do today, but did know anti-depressants can trigger mania. I filled the prescription, but was too afraid to take it.

This was also the time of one of our nation's worst tragedies, when terrorists attacked America on September 11, 2001. Most people who remember 9/11 can recall exactly what they were doing on that day. I was out of work on leave and still had not seen a doctor. I remember feeling this emotional wave of grief come over me as if I had gone into a state of shock.

Scarlett's mother called me to ask if I was watching television. She said, "We've been attacked by terrorists in New York City. Turn your TV on." Then she asked, "Where's Scarlett?"

"Scarlett is in Los Angeles," I replied. "I'll call her to make sure she's safe."

Scarlett spent several days a week traveling for work and happened to be in Los Angeles, stranded because all the flights were grounded. Eventually, she and a colleague rented a car and headed back to Phoenix. We all breathed a sigh of relief when she came home safely.

I turned on the television at the same time the second plane was crashing into the World Trade Center. I thought about how I had recently been to the top floor restaurant and had stayed at the Marriott Hotel that was accessible to the World Trade Center by an escalator. When the buildings came down and the newscasters talked about how the underground subway was destroyed, I knew exactly what they were talking about because I had been there.

The entire tragedy added to my intense emotions of grief and sadness. I had not had time to grieve for everything that had happened that summer. It was all very surreal.

* * *

I was not thrilled to see a doctor, but it was not my first appointment with an outpatient psychiatrist. My first appointment was in Philadelphia after I was released from Johns Hopkins. This doctor told me there was no way I could have bipolar disorder and took all the medications I was prescribed and dumped them in the trash. He said, "Believe me—I am doing you a favor." I never went back to him and was quite honestly very skeptical of psychiatrists.

The psychiatrist I saw in Arizona was definitely a woman of few words. My appointment lasted for about an hour, and she prescribed a fraction of what the doctor in West Virginia had given me. I was to take one small dose every other day. I always wondered if she ever read my medical records. Her diagnosis for me was "bipolar disorder not otherwise specified," which meant she wasn't sure which type of bipolar disorder I had, even though it should have been clear based on my past medical records that I had bipolar disorder type 1 with psychotic features. There was much evidence to suggest that would have been the appropriate diagnosis. And it mattered because the medication regimens are different depending on the severity of symptoms.

I would have liked to have sat with a psychiatrist and traced back everything that had happened to me. It would have been great for someone to explain the symptoms of bipolar disorder and how the medications work to keep a person's mood stable. At this point, I had only come into the system through crisis situations, so this was my first opportunity to have a conversation about what happened.

Except, the conversation never took place.

I did choose to read any books I could find about bipolar disorder, but I didn't see myself in what was being described. It undoubtedly had a lot to do with stigma, denial, and the fact that bipolar disorder symptoms have variations for each person. No one will experience the illness in exactly the same way. This adds to the complexity of a person's treatment plan, making it more difficult and sometimes a lengthy process to find which medications work to control symptoms.

Looking back, I know I was experiencing severe mood swings. Some days I could work, hike, and travel for hours on little or no sleep. Other times I had a hard time putting my feet on the ground to move. I made several life changes during this time, and most were decisions I had to deal with once I became mentally stable again.

* * *

Christmas rolled around, and I decided I would make chocolate chip cookies. I bought a huge bag of Nestle Toll House chocolate chips. I placed it in the pantry and went out of the house for a bit. When I returned, Goldie had eaten the entire bag of chocolate chips, which is horrible for a dog. Within a few days, Goldie died two weeks before Christmas. I felt horribly guilty because I had bought the stupid chocolate chips. I rarely baked or cooked anything, and it made matters worse.

Chance recognized her friend and playmate was gone and was grieving. Goldie's death triggered my depression, and I became very detached and despondent. A couple of weeks later, Scarlett came home from a work trip and said, "I can't stand this sadness anymore. Let's go to the pound and get another dog."

I wasn't really up for a new dog, but Chance and I kind of went along for the ride. We picked out a lab mix and called her Gia. She was a sweet dog, but we couldn't bring her home for a week. It didn't stop Scarlett from driving to the mall.

"What are we doing here?" I asked, knowing in my heart she was going to buy a puppy.

We wandered around the pet store and picked a fluffy yellow lab we called Shasta. She was absolutely beautiful and full of pep. Scarlett carried her out of the store and placed her in my hands for the drive home. With all the grief I was feeling, I didn't want to get attached to yet another pet. The cloud of darkness, depression, and death of loved ones and pets was hovering over my head.

Shasta ended up having a terrible respiratory infection that took weeks to recover from. It turned out Gia had been exposed to distemper at the shelter prior to our bringing her home, and she became ill and died New Year's Day. We'd barely had her a month. I had officially turned off all my emotions and simply tried to survive.

* * *

Without the right combination of medications, it did not take long for me to have another manic episode. It did not help I had left my secure job with the pharmaceutical company and was running our own business—a Quiznos sub shop. The plan was to open several franchises and I would manage them.

A cruel aspect of bipolar disorder is when manic, you're getting things you don't need and getting rid of things you do. I lost many relationships during this time, and it would take years for me to learn how to forgive myself.

I abruptly ended my almost ten-year relationship with Scarlett. I simply left the house one day and never went back except to pack up my things while she was out of town.

That day, I sat on the couch across from where she was sitting and told her, "It's over. I'm leaving."

She was completely caught off guard and suggested, "Aim, let's call your therapist."

"No," I said, and that was pretty much the end of the conversation. Every time I had gotten sick, I threatened to leave the relationship. My anger and irritability was always placed on the doorstep of those I cared about most. Scarlett might have had enough of the bipolar merry-go-round.

Not all my friends lived in Phoenix. Many were scattered throughout the country. When they found out about my unstable mood and dramatic episodes, many faded away from my life. I was also not in the position to maintain friendships—I was struggling to survive.

Even though I was under a doctor's care, I didn't realize I had been experiencing symptoms until I found an online mental health screen for bipolar disorder. After I clicked on the button to submit my answers, the standardized form said, "Based on how you answered the questions, you may be experiencing a bipolar disorder episode. Seek medical attention immediately."

On my way to work one morning I had a conversation with my sister Sherry. She told me the hard truth that I didn't want to admit—I had been ill, and my actions were uncharacteristic.

"What's going on?" Sherry said, very concerned.

"I'm feeling depressed, and I don't even know if I want to live anymore," I said bluntly. "I took this online questionnaire, and it says I'm having an episode."

"Amy, I really think you need to go to the hospital. They can help you," she pleaded.

The fact that Sherry spoke kindly to me made a big difference. In my right mind, I would not have walked away from my home and my relationship and never gone back. But the fact that I never was completely stabilized on the right combination of medications began to have significant implications in my personal and professional life.

For whatever reason, I listened to Sherry that day and asked my longtime friends Marianne and Jenni to help me. I had met them at a church Scarlett and I used to attend, and they were steadfast in their willingness to help me. I called them one morning and told them I thought I'd been sick, and I needed to go to the hospital. Within minutes, they were at my door helping me make arrangements to get help. They both had so much compassion for me, and they still do. They are truly great friends and awesome people.

Scarlett was out of town, but Jenni tracked her down for the healthcare insurance information. She kept me on her policy until I found an employer who provided healthcare benefits.

One of the hardest things about locating suitable mental health treatment is finding a good fit with the doctor, keeping in mind that he or she is also human. They aren't mind readers, and they can't treat me if I am not being honest with them about my symptoms or how I'm feeling. But how could I be honest about those things if I didn't understand my illness?

When I took myself voluntarily to the hospital for inpatient care, I discovered there are huge differences in treatment facilities. The place I went had a swimming pool and basketball court. I had excellent care and was given medication that is textbook for bipolar disorder. If only I had stayed with the treatment.

I stayed in the hospital for about five days. I had four friends who came to visit, each one reassuring me that it was okay that I had a mental illness, and my life was worth living. All I had to do was take the medication. I understood what they were saying; I just wished it were that simple.

It was odd not having Scarlett there to support me. She had been my rock through good times and bad. While in the hospital, I came to the sobering realization of what I had done. I would carry the hurt, guilt, and longing in my heart for the great life my undertreated bipolar disorder had destroyed.

This is where shame and regret began to build up over the years. I had these opportunities to embrace my diagnosis and learn how to manage the illness instead of letting it uncontrollably disrupt my life. Unfortunately, this is not uncommon for many people who live with bipolar disorder. In my case, it was not about liking the manic highs, it was about self-stigma, denial, and the awful side effects of the medications. I had seen the significant weight gain my sister experienced, and I did not want that to happen to me. I sincerely didn't understand the implications of what would happen if I continued on this path.

At this time in my life, bipolar disorder was running the show. I wasn't able to make good decisions. I take responsibility for being unable to maintain relationships, friendships, and making poor business decisions. For many years, I beat myself up because I believed I was even more accountable because I had refused to accept that I had a mental illness, and I paid a significant price because of stigma and my unwillingness to accept that I have bipolar disorder.

In spite of my mental health challenges, I did experience times without symptoms. Doctors would call this "periods of normalcy."

By this time, I was working in my own business, but there is a saying about real estate, and the same is true with sandwich shops—location, location, location. We didn't have a good location, and there was too much competition for the same type of business within a few miles' radius. Each time the franchisor opened another store, our sales would go down thirty percent. After a year, the writing was on the wall, and new owners would have to be found.

I had two business partners, but I managed to alienate both of them. My relationship with Scarlett was over, and Danielle and I fought over just about everything. Even though it was a direct cause of my unmanaged bipolar disorder, and they knew I was struggling, they didn't know how to help me. The stress from working sixteen-hour days was contributing to my symptoms. It wasn't easy for them to handle my high levels of irritability, a common symptom of bipolar disorder. Eventually, we sold the business, and I returned to work in the pharmaceutical industry.

While I was managing a business and dealing with my mental health challenges, my family stood by me and helped as much as they could. We were also dealing with the deaths of five loved ones who were all integral parts of our lives. The losses started with my father, and two weeks later my Uncle Forest, who was more like my grandfather, died after a long battle with dementia. Shortly after that, my Aunt Patty passed away. There was never enough time to grieve before our very close cousin, Neva, who lived until she was almost one hundred, died.

In November 2002, my Aunt Mary Francis died from a glioblastoma brain tumor. Even though she was eighty-two, her loss was very hard on the family, probably compounded with having lost so many people in such a short period of time. A few weeks later, another cousin, Ted, died from brain cancer.

Dealing with so much loss caused my emotions to simply go numb. I could not feel anything. It was like going through the motions every day just trying to survive. It certainly did not help that I was struggling with my own mental health challenges and facing the aftermath of decisions I made when I was not stable.

I continued to learn lessons about putting my head down and forging onward with life. It helped to work through my grieving in counseling sessions, which gave me some additional coping tools. Believe me, it took everything I had to keep on functioning.

Often, I tend to treat myself very harshly, even though I know I did the best I could with the situations I faced. When things got really tough, I learned the only way to the other side was to go through the pain. Some days were easier than others, but when given a mountain of challenges, survival becomes the ultimate strategy.

The doctor I was seeing left her private practice for another opportunity. I was given a referral, and I continued my appointments and took the medications as prescribed. We had to come to a compromise over which medications I could tolerate and still function at a higher level. The regimen worked for a few years.

Despite my personal challenges, I was given many opportunities, but sustaining a long period of wellness was impossible without the proper treatment.

After selling the business and returning to the pharmaceutical industry, I recovered, and over the next few years I lived rather peacefully. I traveled significantly and enjoyed several business trips to Hawaii and other gorgeous places.

My greatest joys were my four-legged friends, Chance, Shasta, and Buddy—two Labradors and a beagle. After my breakup with Scarlett, we agreed I would keep the dogs. Shortly thereafter, I rescued Buddy. They were all best friends. When I was out of town, my good friend Glenda would come and stay at my house and take care of my dogs. Our routine was a daily hike and a swim in the pool. The hikes were often four or five miles, sometimes longer. It helped me to manage my stress, and ultimately my illness.

Things became more difficult when my employer wanted me to cover ten states in the Western Region as a marketing director, and bipolar or no bipolar, there was no way I could keep up that pace. The intense travel was very hard on my mental and physical health. I had always traveled for work, but leaving on a Monday morning and returning on Thursday was not the lifestyle I wanted to live. Making arrangements for someone to take care of my dogs, getting up at 5:00 a.m., rushing to the airport to catch a flight, standing in long security lines, sitting in the middle seat on a packed airplane, taking the shuttle to get a rental car, and then fighting the traffic in Los Angeles, San Francisco, or New Jersey grew old very quickly. It sounds like fun on the outside looking in, but it is exhausting and not something I enjoyed.

In addition, the company I worked for had recently been through a downsizing, resulting in massive layoffs, and the people who were left resented those of us who were hired to take the place of some of their old friends and colleagues. It was no fun to work in an environment where half the people wished I wasn't there.

I left the company a little less than two years later and started working for a biotechnology company based out of Phoenix. Along with dealing with a mental health disorder, I had to cope with the severe pain from endometriosis and polycystic ovarian syndrome.

A few months before I changed jobs again, I had to have a hysterectomy, and after my surgery, the hormonal changes affected my mood badly. I have no evidence that changes in hormones can trigger a bipolar episode, but from what I experienced, I believe this made my illness worse. I found myself falling into another very deep depression and had difficulty finding the motivation to work every day. It became harder to get out and exercise, even though it was something I loved to do.

In January 2006, despite having changed jobs because of the travel schedule, I ended up traveling more with the new job, and that proved to be very hard on my mental health. It wasn't uncommon for me to be in two or three different cities in a week. In one year, I had logged over 100,000 air miles. The most challenging trips were the cross-country flights where frequent time changes interrupted my ability to sleep. The less sleep I had, the more difficult it was to manage my moods. Primarily, I struggled with the ups and downs of bipolar disorder. I went from having mild mania, irritability, and a bit of paranoia, to being depressed. Nothing severe enough for anyone to notice, and if they did, no one ever said anything to me about it, but I was going down a very bad path and I was losing insight.

I started to isolate myself from friends and family. It wasn't a conscious decision; it was only because I was struggling. But the more isolated I made myself, the more difficult my struggles became, so no one was around me enough to notice that I was spiraling right into the middle of another mental health crisis. I had always been close to my family and rarely had any type of conflict, so it was extremely unusual for me to behave in an adversarial way. The high levels of irritability caused friction, and after spending the holidays with my family at my home in Phoenix, I found myself at odds with everyone, including my mom.

Mom would call me, and I stopped answering her calls. Being the persistent woman she is, she would follow up her call with a lengthy email telling me I needed to see a doctor and that something was wrong with me. I believe it was a mother's sixth sense. She always knew my moods well and could tell if something was bothering me. Even during my adolescent years, if something was wrong, she would point it out and ask me to talk about it.

One day I came home from work and checked my personal email. Mom had written me the following email on November 4, 2005. I found it with my old journals.

"Dear Amy,

It is a terrible thing when we can't accept the fact we have a mental illness. It is no different than a physical one. You take your medicine and work with professional people to help you work through it. You need support and understanding. You were doing so good. Have a good job, everything going well for you. Why do you want to keep doing this to yourself? It is a chemical imbalance. I love you and support you all I can. We are all proud of you and all your accomplishments. I loved coming out to Phoenix and spending time with you. We have always been so close. Please get help. You're headed for trouble. Take it from one who knows. Use your intelligence to recognize the fact you have Bipolar Illness which is a chemical imbalance and you need help. Stop trying to deny that fact.

I love you,

Mom."

I always wanted a crystal ball, but I believe what my mother wrote was a prophecy. As if she had predicted the future was going to bring bigger challenges, higher rollercoasters, and difficult situations. I wish I had listened.

There were a lot of moments in between my struggles when I could pull myself together. On one of these occasions, I gave a talk to a group of students. The Olympic Committee would ask Olympic alumni to speak at certain engagements, and I had agreed to talk to a group of elementary school students. I remember teaching them a song about the "doubters" and how to "stomp out the doubters" that I had learned in 4-H as a kid. I would one day have to learn to take my own advice.

Chapter 12

One Long, Hot, Dangerous Day

One of my last pleasant memories was during May 2006 when a friend and I made a trip to Las Vegas to see Madonna. We had a great time and an enjoyable weekend. Who would have ever thought it would turn into one of the worst years of my life? In January, I had a friend tell me she was certain I did not have bipolar disorder, and I should not be taking the medication. They were the words I wanted to hear because, even though I had continued to take the medication and see a doctor, I had not yet given in to accepting the diagnosis. This was one of the biggest mistakes I had made.

June 25, 2006.

I'll never forget that day because it's my mom's birthday. I had become really defiant with my family. I barely talked to them, and my unusual behavior alarmed them. But I was 2000 miles away, and there was not much they could do to help me.

I had stopped taking the medication I'd been prescribed, which even in the small amount had kept me out of the hospital. But after six months of moving fast and furious, I had a manic and a psychotic episode.

I thought everyone was out to get me. No one could reach me because I was having a psychotic episode. Psychosis is defined by having delusions where what you think is not based in reality, or hallucinations where you are either seeing, hearing, smelling, or tasting things that are not there. My episodes came in the form of delusions. It built gradually, starting with a lot of paranoia. My usual insecurities became things I obsessed over.

For example, if I flew into a city and worked with one of my colleagues, if she was using her BlackBerry to answer email or text other peers, I thought they were conversing about me.

I felt a deep sense of scrutiny, and some of it may have been real, but some of it was my paranoia running wild. It is quite natural for employees to talk about management. In fact, I was in a relatively high-profile role, but my mental health challenges were making it more difficult to be confident. My mind raced from one thought to another about how people were talking about me, and I always assumed it was something bad.

On a manic whim, I packed my three dogs in the car to take a trip to Wyoming. I drove for more than thirteen hours before deciding to turn around. I stayed up all through the night and grew so exhausted I finally stopped at a hotel. After I checked in and went to my room, I became filled with fear. I was scared of every little noise. After only a few minutes, I left the hotel.

I drove back to Phoenix, and at around four o'clock in the morning, I stopped at Danielle's house. She welcomed me and the dogs in, but said, "Amy, what are you doing at this early hour? Are you okay?"

I told her I was fine and wanted to come and visit her. "I've missed you," I said. I had no concept of time or how inappropriate it was to show up on someone's doorstep at four in the morning. I had no idea I had lost touch with reality.

I stayed for a short time, and then got back in the car and started driving. The dogs were accustomed to traveling. They all curled up in the back seat of the white Cadillac Escalade and slept while I drove around. Even in my failing mental state, I always managed to make sure I let them out of the car for breaks and that they had access to a water bowl.

I strongly believe Danielle knew something was wrong with me but wasn't sure what to do to help. Scarlett had asked Danielle to come and stay with me when I had a manic episode in the past and Scarlett had to attend an out of town meeting. Danielle was aware I had bipolar disorder.

Hours passed as I drove around, fading in and out of reality. I tried to find my way back to Danielle's house, but I couldn't remember how to get there. Finally, I stopped my Escalade in the middle of the road and got out, leaving the door open and the keys in the ignition, and started wandering the streets of Phoenix singing religious songs.

My dogs walked along beside me as they always did when we took our hikes, except this time I had unknowingly put their safety at risk. Walking in the middle of the street, without the dogs on leashes, and with morning rush hour traffic approaching, I had truly become a "danger to myself or others." I was walking in front of moving cars, the people, thankfully, nice enough to stop. Though motorists were honking their horns, no one attempted to help me. In my delusional state, I thought the world was coming to an end, and I was an angel who could walk through the cars.

Two police officers eventually arrived, and as soon as I saw them, I grabbed my dogs and sat down in the front yard of someone's house.

"What are you doing walking in the middle of the street?" one officer asked.

"Just taking my dogs for a walk," I replied in a very matter-of-fact manner.

"Where do you live?"

"I live in Paradise Valley." Paradise Valley is one of the most expensive zip codes in Arizona. I suspect if I had said any other area, he may have treated me differently. It has also entered my mind that how they handled the situation might have changed if I had been African-American, Latino, or homeless. I know I was fortunate because of my socioeconomic position.

The officers loaded my dogs and me in the back of their cruiser, one of them drove my Escalade, and they took me home. They called a crisis team to come to my house to evaluate me.

Generally, a crisis team consists of mental health professionals, sometimes psychiatrists, nurses, social workers, or other mental health specialists. Two young people, probably in their early twenties, sat at the kitchen table with me and "observed" my behavior. They were definitely not nurses or doctors.

I was very calm and didn't say much to them. They never asked me any questions about what I had been doing or if I was hearing voices, seeing things that weren't there, or what kind of thoughts I had. Not even a question about why I had been walking in the middle of the street. At one point, I left the kitchen, took a shower, played the piano for a little while, and that was it.

They concluded I was mentally stable and not a danger to myself or others, as if it was perfectly normal that I had walked around in the middle of the street, singing religious songs, letting my dogs run around without leashes. I honestly don't know what they were thinking, but it really drives the point home—this was another opportunity to get me some help before the situation escalated. Sometimes people with severe mental illness are vulnerable to the very system that is supposed to help them. In this case, I feel like I was a victim. I needed help, but other people should have made sure I got the help necessary.

After everyone left the house, I was alone. My psychosis continued to worsen, and I began singing religious songs at the top of my lungs outside in the back yard. A former Marine who took care of my pool came into the yard while I was out there. He was about 6'4" and extremely nice, and I always talked to him when I was home. But that day, I wanted to pick a fight.

Each time I experienced psychosis, I was never aware of what I was doing at the time. I don't know why, but I ran up to him and pushed him. Maybe I felt threatened. He instinctively picked me up and threw me in the pool. I started laughing. I had no understanding of what I was doing or what was happening around me.

Danielle, who I visited earlier that morning, showed up in my back yard. I tried pulling her into the swimming pool, but she yelled at me to let go of her arm.

"Amy, I don't want to swim," she said and kind of laughed.

"Come on, Danielle. It will be fun."

"No, Amy," she shouted. "Let go of my arm."

Danielle was a little taller than I was, just under six feet and extremely fit. As I let go of her hand, she fell down and started screaming for the Marine to call the police.

The police arrived quickly and found me swimming in the pool. When I saw them coming through the patio doors, I jumped up out of the pool and asked if they wanted to swim.

One of the officers, with authority, said, "No, we don't want to swim. You're coming with us."

I sat down on the ground and folded my arms. The officers picked me up and dragged me about twenty yards through desert landscaping, which consisted largely of cacti. They tried forcing me into the back of the police car, but I resisted. I had taken a self-defense course and I was trained how to place my feet on the ground and crawl backward from an abductor. In this case, the police were my abductors. Even though the handcuffs were secured behind my back, I managed to brace myself with my legs and not allow them to put me in the car. I was screaming, "Please don't hurt me." After a lengthy battle, they eventually called for the paramedics.

As my luck would have it, one of the paramedics was the husband of the corporate recruiter who had helped me get back into the pharmaceutical industry. Needless to say, she would never help me find a job again. I can't say I blame her.

The paramedics took my vital signs and wiped my face with a cool towel, and then left. I don't remember them asking me anything. Not even my name. It was like I was a criminal and not a person having a mental health crisis. The officers told me to get in the back of the police car, which I did without incident, and they took me to jail.

I was placed in a small holding cell with my hands cuffed to a cement block. I shivered because I was soaking wet from being in the pool, wearing a t-shirt and shorts. I sang *Amazing Grace* at the top of my lungs.

The strangest thing was the police officers wrote in their report that I had called myself the devil. It could not have been further from the truth. All my delusions were very consistent. I was either the Holy Spirit or someone with religious powers sent here to do good. But explaining something like that in a court of law would have been impossible. Imagine saying to the judge, "The police officers lied on their report. I would never call myself the devil. I believe I'm on God's team."

Even though that was true, I never got the chance to tell anyone because I doubted they would give any credibility to a person with mental illness, even if I had recovered. Most people don't understand severe mental illness, let alone psychosis and the fact that a person can regain sanity.

After I wore myself out singing, I asked the officer to uncuff my hands from the cement block. He told me to behave and he would do it.

Some time passed and the police loaded me into a van and took me to an outpatient crisis treatment facility. I use the word "treatment" loosely. It was one of the worst places I had ever been. There were about five beds in total in separate rooms, and the rest of the sitting area was a big room for the patients with recliner chairs that didn't fully recline. There were more people than chairs. It was packed and not at all therapeutic, a poor excuse for a mental health treatment facility.

Even though I had just experienced a severe delusional episode, I was only kept in the clinic for a little over twenty-four hours before they released me. Once again, in my opinion, this was malpractice. Sometimes, the bigger the city, the worse the mental health treatment. That is if you call treatment throwing a handful of medications at someone who is not in their right mind and expecting them to comply. I believe releasing me early from the treatment facility had more to do with their lack of beds than it did with what was best for me. My mental state was so bad that I wasn't able to tell them I had great insurance. But it didn't seem to matter what my health coverage was. It only mattered that they needed a bed for someone who was in worse shape than I was, if that's even possible to envision.

When I got to the treatment facility, I called my mom to tell her where I was. She called my cousin Christy, and the two of them flew to Phoenix to help me. She and Mom stayed with me for the rest of the summer, taking turns cooking dinner and taking care of my dogs, while I slowly regained my sanity.

I cycled back and forth on the bipolar mood chart. The mania led me to one of my biggest spending sprees ever. I bought a thirty-four-foot motor home online and picked it up the following day. Christy and I took a cross-country trip from Arizona to Florida, making the most of a difficult situation.

When I look back, I have to laugh at some of the things I did, things I would never do if I had been stable.

* * *

As you can imagine, I was mortified over what happened. There is a great deal of vulnerability in writing a story like this, but I write it because there is such a tremendous misunderstanding about psychosis and the people with mental illness who encounter law enforcement. I do not fit the stereotype of a person who has experienced psychosis, and yet about seventy percent of people who have bipolar disorder experience psychotic episodes during periods of depression or mania.

Not everyone who has bipolar disorder or who experiences a psychotic episode will have an encounter with the police. Because I lost touch with reality in the form of delusions, it did make me a danger to myself or others, and not knowing I was ill meant I couldn't tell caseworkers what I was thinking. In my case, I believe there was ample opportunity to get help for me in a respectful and dignified manner. At the end of the day, though, I am ultimately responsible for my own behavior whether I was sane or not.

None of us, regardless of socioeconomic level or success, is immune to mental illness and the devastating effects it can have on one's life. I had many opportunities to get help and learn to manage my illness before getting to this level of crisis. I've been challenged over the years to learn how to let go of the blame, and there certainly is plenty to go around, but who is accountable when a person cannot think clearly? Who is responsible for helping someone with a mental illness who has lost touch with reality? What could other people have done to help me? Why didn't anyone explain to me that if I didn't get the proper treatment, there was a high likelihood that I could seriously jeopardize my life? Whose responsibility was it to help me comprehend the extent of what I was dealing with?

It was my accountability for having stopped seeing my psychiatrist and not taking the proper medications. It wasn't as if I didn't have access to care, because I did. The number one reason I didn't continue with my treatment plan was the stigma and a defiant attitude that I was not going to be included with "the mentally ill" because "those people" are discriminated against. Who can honestly say that's a group I want to belong to? And yet I needed help in understanding the ramifications of bipolar disorder. I know it would have made a difference.

None of this is an excuse; it's simply my reality. It also happened many years ago, long before social media became so popular. Now it's relatively easy to find outspoken, confident mental health advocates who live with bipolar disorder. It makes a difference to know you are not alone and to have access to those who can relate to the symptoms I was experiencing.

Chapter 13

One Step Forward, Two Steps Back

The consequences of my untreated bipolar disorder continued to paint my life with sporadic decisions and over the top risks. The implications of my alternating moods began to knock me off my life's path.

In spite of my deteriorated mental health, I was only hospitalized that summer for a total of five days. My brief hospitalizations led me to seek outpatient psychiatric treatment. I knew something was wrong, but I was not well enough to grasp the gravity of the situation. And, unfortunately, I was diagnosed with post-traumatic stress disorder (PTSD) by one of the physicians in the hospital and given medication to treat it. I made an appointment with a psychiatrist, but it was three months before she could see me.

By the time I was stabilized enough to know I needed treatment, I saw a psychiatric nurse practitioner who prescribed some medications for me. She worked with the counselor I had been seeing for PTSD. When the PTSD symptoms started, that prompted me to see a therapist in Phoenix who suggested I participate in trauma therapy. I was having flashbacks of various things that had happened to me, including the time I'd been restrained for fourteen hours in the hospital in Philadelphia.

I was also having flashbacks of watching my father die. A few days before he passed, the blood vessels in his legs looked like they were going to explode. Then they would recede, only to have it happen again. The last time he took a breath, his whole body looked like a web of broken blood vessels. It was incredibly difficult to watch, let alone close his eyes after he died.

I didn't realize the impact of PTSD until I was on an airplane from Phoenix to Denver and I began having a flashback of being tied to a hospital bed, feeling as if I was suffocating. In my experience, once the intrusive memories began, it was very difficult to know what might trigger a flashback. It seemed like anything could trigger one for me, but if I did not get enough sleep I became more vulnerable.

As soon as the plane took off, I found my way to a restroom and stayed in there for the entire two-hour flight. I believe the trauma therapy made the bipolar disorder worse. I felt as if the scabs of wounds had torn off and the scars were not allowed to form, and both conditions became very complicated to treat. I ended up in therapy for six years, from 2005 to 2011, and my mental health condition only got worse.

The summer of 2006, I took a leave of absence from my job and spent the next few months recovering. When the summer ended, I decided to leave Phoenix and return east to be closer to my family.

I had applied for a position with a medical device company in Pittsburgh. I took a red-eye flight to Pittsburgh and changed clothes in an airport restroom for the job interview. There was a lot of competition for the position, but the company made it a point to bring in people who had grown up in the greater Pittsburgh area and wanted to return home. Even though I grew up an hour away from Pittsburgh, I still qualified.

I was offered the job and set out in my thirty-four-foot recreational vehicle across the country with my three dogs and Mom. Moving from the sunny Arizona desert to the cloudy, green, rolling hills of Western Pennsylvania was a shock to my system. The average number of sunny days in Phoenix is about three hundred, and in Pittsburgh about seventy. The lack of sunshine would eventually impact my moods and trigger the worst depressive episode of my life.

After five months of working in a cubicle, I realized I was not cut out to sit behind a desk. Most of my previous jobs had been in field sales, which meant I traveled around to various places and wasn't confined to a desk. This was helpful in managing mild symptoms of hypomania. The extra energy could be used to work harder, and the exercise helped to keep me stable. But sitting behind a desk increased my anxiety and made me feel like a caged animal that needed to run.

After a few months, I contacted the biotechnology company I had worked for in Phoenix to see if they had any positions available in Pittsburgh. Coincidentally, they were looking for someone to cover five states in the mid-Atlantic region, and because I had left the company with a good reputation, I was rehired. Even in the midst of my struggles, I was somehow able to perform at a high level in my work.

I had many business trips all over the country. One that stands out in my mind was a trip at Disney World. A friend of mine from Phoenix asked if she could meet up with me in Orlando, and share my hotel room with me. While I worked, she enjoyed the gorgeous hotel and surrounding area.

When we were getting ready to go our separate ways, she looked rather distressed and said, "I can't be friends with a schizophrenic!"

I was completely caught off guard. "I don't have schizophrenia," I replied. "And even if I don't, that's really rude."

She shrugged and walked out the door. I never talked to her again.

That was one of the few times anyone has made a disparaging comment to my face. I'm sure there have been plenty of conversations behind my back, and perhaps I've been the target of a "she's crazy" statement or two. I don't worry too much about what other people think about me. Some folks should consider themselves lucky they've never had to deal with a cruel mental illness.

* * *

Shortly after accepting the position in Pittsburgh, I received a certified letter in the mail and assumed it was about the Quiznos I had sold in Phoenix. I remember that day like it was yesterday. I was sitting outside the post office when I opened the letter.

I was being charged with a crime for what happened on that hot and dangerous day in Phoenix.

The police officer said in his report that after I had asked him to swim in the pool with me, I hit him. There is no question I was not in my right mind, but I know I never hit him. When the officers told me to come with them, I sat down on the ground and folded my arms. I was charged with aggravated assault against a law enforcement officer and resisting arrest.

After everything I had been through, the one thing I was not was a criminal, and now I was being thrust into the criminal justice system because I was not taken for mental health treatment after I first had contact with the police officers in downtown Phoenix. The situation was allowed to escalate and, though I am accountable for my actions, I did not deserve to be treated like a criminal.

Sadly, I have since learned that I am one of millions of people who live with mental illness who have encountered the criminal justice system. In fact, jails have become the new mental hospital of the 21st century. It's easy to see how a mental health crisis can escalate without the proper care. Based on figures from the Bureau of Justice Statistics and the U.S. Department of Health and Human Services, there are currently three times more seriously mentally ill people in jails and prisons than in hospitals in the U.S., with the ratio being nearly ten to one in Arizona and Nevada. According to the National Alliance on Mental Illness, serious mental illness is defined by such conditions as schizophrenia, bipolar disorder, psychotic disorders, or major depression.

Most people who have a mental illness will never have any interaction with the law. In fact, there are more than sixty million people living with a mental illness. I'm far from being alone when it comes to the criminal justice system. However, I'm still in the minority.

For someone who's had relatively little interaction of any type with the law, with the exception of a couple speeding tickets, the criminal justice system is daunting and scary. In my experience, the outcome of charges and convictions depends on what type of attorney a person has and how much understanding the court has about mental illness.

In many places across the country, mental health courts serve a purpose similar to a drug court, with the primary goal of making sure a person gets treatment. Unless someone has committed a heinous crime, I believe treatment is by far the more humane option than jail or prison.

I had to return to Phoenix to appear in court. I was dressed in one of my best business suits with my mother by my side. The judge looked at me like, "Is this the same person described in this police report?"

The attorney I hired said she would meet me before the court appearance. I paid her $5000, and she only spoke to me for less than three minutes. I never had a chance to see the police report until minutes before I went before a judge. My attorney told me it was best if I pleaded no contest to the crimes, because the best possible outcome was to have one misdemeanor offense. No contest was not admitting guilt, but accepting the plea bargain agreement. The prosecuting attorney dropped the resisting arrest charge. While I was happy not to have a felony on my record, I still felt as if I did not deserve a criminal conviction of any kind.

I didn't speak in court other than to answer the question, "Ms. Gamble, how do you plead?"

I answered, "No contest."

I felt strongly about not saying I was guilty of a crime I knew I didn't commit. To this day, I am virtually certain I didn't slap the police officer. In all my psychotic episodes, I had never been violent. If I pled not guilty, the case would have gone to trial. There was no guarantee the jury would find me not guilty. I didn't want to take the risk, because if found guilty by the jury, the sentence would have included jail time and possibly two felonies on my criminal record.

I ended up with a misdemeanor record and was fortunate enough that when my employer did a background check, they understood the incident was related to my mental health.

They told me they would still hire me, but if it ever happened again, I'd be fired.

My punishment was one year of probation, which was beyond stressful and contributed to further degradation of my mental health. I could travel for work, but I was not allowed beyond a ten-mile radius of my home otherwise. I had to call my probation officer whenever I left Pittsburgh and again when I arrived at my destination. I would say, "Hi, this is Amy Gamble, and I want to let you know I'm boarding the plane at the Pittsburgh airport," later followed by, "This is Amy Gamble, and I want to let you know I just checked into the Ritz Carlton in Philadelphia." I felt like I was living in a fog. How could I be at the Ritz Carlton one moment and be confined to my home the next?

A few years later, I hired another attorney to have my record "set aside." Melody indicated how sorry she was this had happened to me. I wished I could have found her the first time around, as I believe my court case would have had a different outcome.

In 2011, Melody wrote the court a several-page letter explaining what had happened to me, along with an application to expunge the conviction. Eventually, the judge ruled in my favor. But the pressure of the entire experience would contribute to one of the darkest periods in my life.

I had so much guilt for not taking responsibility for my illness. I beat myself up thinking I should have known to take my medication to keep my condition in check. It would take me years to overcome the impact of what I saw as my poor decision-making. However, in retrospect, I truly believe the system failed me, and I know I am not alone.

But this experience also fuels my passion for delivering mental health awareness presentations. I speak from a place of genuine interest in the well-being of people who are struggling with mental illness and don't understand the implications of not finding the proper treatment regimen. I know firsthand what can happen, and though others may never experience the extreme situations I have, tragic outcomes can be avoided. Not everyone will end up in a legal jam like I did, but much of the suffering can be avoided if the proper treatment is found. Lives can be saved with a simple message that says help is available and treatment works, and there is no shame in having a mental illness.

* * *

In March of 2008, I was released from my probation period, and I took a week off from work to see my friend, Diane, from Colorado Springs, who I met while training for the Olympics. She was on spring break, and we decided to meet up in Las Vegas.

Shortly after I returned home, I began having depressive symptoms that I couldn't shake. I was sleeping longer and longer. I stopped doing any exercise. I could no longer concentrate on my work, and I had to go on short-term disability. Stress, guilt, isolation, and situations that overwhelmed my coping skills took me down. I was also living alone, and I did not know anyone in the Pittsburgh area. My mother, Shelley, and niece Natalie were the only people who visited me, and they all lived almost two hours away. The only one left standing after my illness started to get worse was my mother.

The only bright spot in my life during this time were my three dogs and a cat I had adopted. If it weren't for the unconditional love of my pets, I would not be here today. When I struggled with suicidal thoughts, I would ask myself, "Who will take care of your animals?" I believed no one would love them as much as I did, and that mutual love saved my life.

My employer wasn't very supportive of me taking time off and kept asking when I would return to work. In all fairness, the economy was experiencing a recession, and the company was owned by venture capital investors. Their tolerance for risky investments in a biotechnology industry that wasn't making a profit was low and soon abandoned. Many of the people I worked with were laid off, but I was one of the fortunate ones who kept their jobs.

But depression doesn't happen at convenient times. It's like any other illness. When a person gets sick and can't function, it's never a good time. Additionally, I was still dealing with the flashbacks. They were like a wave that kept knocking me over. Anything negative from the past was free game for the flashbacks. I would start shaking and my body would jerk. Sometimes I would smell things that weren't there. I remember a time when I tasted blood, probably from the severe nosebleeds I had as a child. I was hallucinating. I was exhausted after reliving these dramatically negative events. I was trying to learn coping skills to manage the flashbacks, but everything was happening so quickly I couldn't keep up.

Any emotional trauma in my life was viewed in my brain like watching a movie at the theater. It would start with jerky movement of my head, and my eyes would blink rapidly. After I talked myself out of the flashback and into the present, I often welled up with uncontrollable crying. More often I found myself lying in bed with my hand over my head in utter despair. A combination of PTSD and bipolar disorder created the perfect storm.

I was under the care of Dr. Martin, a psychiatrist, and Jackie, a therapist, who were treating me for PTSD. I don't know if they read my medical records or if they just didn't believe I had bipolar disorder, but the lack of appropriate medications caused me to regress into the worst condition I had ever experienced. And every time I got a new medication, I would gain twenty pounds. By the time I raised my head and could function somewhat normally, I had gained eighty pounds from the bipolar depression and the side effects of the medications.

In December of 2008, I voluntarily admitted myself for inpatient care. I decided that since I was under a doctor's care and continued to get worse, I might benefit from a second opinion and inpatient care. By this time, I was experiencing suicidal thoughts on a daily basis and couldn't stop them. I felt as if I had made a mess of my entire life. I believed everyone would be better off without me. The emotional pain was so intense I wanted to escape it. I felt as if I had become damaged goods, and the hopelessness was overwhelming. Inpatient care was a last resort, but it helped me get on the right track.

The doctor in the hospital knew immediately that I had bipolar disorder and changed all my medications. For the third time in my life, I was given textbook medications to treat bipolar disorder. The side effect from one of the medications was so bad I couldn't tolerate it, and I eventually stopped taking the drug. When I saw Dr. Martin after my inpatient stay, she was shocked they'd changed my medications and asked me why they had. I had no answers for her question.

Despite my continuing decline under Dr. Martin's care, I kept my appointments and stayed with her for five years. I suppose this is why I'm so adamant about finding the proper doctor, one who will have an open dialogue with me but won't rely on me to determine what medications I need or don't need. There is a fine line between having an open dialogue and trusting the doctor to prescribe what she believes is the best possible option. It's hard for me to believe my condition continued to get worse under a doctor's care, but this is the nature of a mental health condition. There isn't a quick-fix medication that will solve the problems. Sometimes it takes years of hard work to achieve a mentally well state of mind.

At forty-two years old, while I was in trauma therapy, one of the books I read suggested buying a video recorder and taping my thoughts and feelings. I now have more than two months of daily recordings. Whenever I view the videos, I can't believe my psychiatrist did not recommend inpatient care. I could have benefitted from appropriate treatment, and it might have prevented me from collapsing.

Chapter 14

What I Did On My Summer Vacation

After spending several days in my house, I decided to take a trip to the beach. I was taking four medications at this point, yet I wasn't completely stabilized. My emotions were like third degree burns on my body. The flashbacks were bringing to the forefront of my mind every negative experience I had lived through. No one wants to keep relieving painful events. The memories played over and over again, like listening to the same song fifty times in a row. But I continued to fight and hope for a positive outcome.

During a doctor's appointment before I left town, I told Dr. Martin I thought I needed an anti-psychotic. The flashbacks were causing me to hallucinate.

"Noooo, Amy. Really?" she asked, like I was some kind of failure for needing this class of drug. It was one of the strangest reactions I'd ever had from a doctor.

I looked at her and said, "Absolutely."

She should have known what medications would help me, but never once did she suggest an anti-psychotic. She gave me a prescription for a drug which added twenty-five pounds to me in a month, never once warning of the side effects. It seemed like I couldn't win.

Shortly after my appointment, I took off in my RV with my three dogs, not telling anyone where I was going. I'm not sure I knew myself what my final destination would be.

My first stop was in Harpers Ferry, West Virginia, where I watched hikers shuffle along the Appalachian Trail. It's beautiful country. I spent a couple of nights in the mountains then headed south to the Outer Banks in North Carolina where I stayed a few nights in a KOA Campground right next to the beach. I was hoping the change of scenery would jump start me into mental healthiness, but as an old book once said, "Wherever you go, there you are." As many times as I changed my location, I could not escape the turmoil of being mentally confused. The only things that would ultimately heal me were a proper medication regimen, time, patience, and a desire to get well. As someone once told me, "Recovery is in the details."

At the end of my stay along the coast, I started driving west, and as I crossed a bridge, I made a split-second decision to drive to Las Vegas. My first stop was Asheville, North Carolina. I have a video recording of me interviewing the gentleman who owned the KOA Campground. Even in some of my most challenging emotional times, I somehow managed to find a bit of fun. I hiked with my dogs and enjoyed the breathtaking scenery of the mountains.

I wasn't thinking practically about how long it would take to drive across the country. It ended up taking over thirty-eight hours to make the trip. Did I have enough supplies? Should I really be traveling without telling anyone where I was going? What about work? How would they feel if they knew I was taking an extended vacation while on disability?

Mania. It does not lend itself to practical thinking. Fleeting thoughts and grandiose plans make for a lethal combination when reality sets in.

One of my most memorable moments of the trip was when the dogs and I stayed the night at a RV park in Williams, Arizona. For some reason, there were a large number of kids there. I would put my dogs on leashes and walk through the park. The kids would run up to me and ask if they could pet the dogs. I noticed the park had a basketball court, and many of the older kids were shooting at the basket. I walked up to the edge of the court and asked, "Would you like for me to teach you how to shoot?"

"Yes!" they all screamed wildly, jumping up and down.

I spent the next couple of hours working with the kids on how to shoot a basketball. Perhaps it was an omen of how I would end up teaching and coaching basketball to boys and girls.

I stayed in Las Vegas for a few days. I even visited my old friend David. Retrospectively, I think he knew I was not quite balanced, but he welcomed me and the dogs into his home. We visited for a while, and then I went back to the campground.

Traveling home was a bit of an adventure. I went through the mountains in Colorado, taking a side trip to Breckenridge. I thought the RV was going to blow an engine making the steep climb up the mountains, going about ten miles per hour with the gas pedal pressed all the way to the floor.

When I finally got to the top, I took my video camera and made a movie with a shining rainbow stretching across the mountains in the background. In one direction, the sun was glimmering over a mountain range. In the other direction, there was a wicked storm brewing. I looked into the camera and said, "Thank God for my miracle!" Watching that video today, I would say I had a prophecy, because in a few years I was going to need more than one miracle.

One of the most memorable parts of the trip was a stop at a pet store in Missouri. I had been thinking about adopting a cat, so when I made my way through the store and came upon a black and white six-week-old kitten, I had to have him. I bought the necessary cat supplies and headed for the RV. Mr. Kitty would go on to become best friends with his new four-legged counterparts. I would often find him sleeping, curled up on the belly of one of my three dogs. He lives a wonderful life in the hills of West Virginia. Trained like a dog, he still follows behind me as we take walks and comes running when I whistle for him. He was a positive highlight of my trip and a bright shining star in the midst of all the darkness.

While I was away, I contacted a corporate recruiter to ask about other companies that might be hiring. I was by no means fit for work, but I can't discount the drive I had to take care of myself.

Little did I know, the company I was working for was monitoring my email. They rerouted my email to someone in corporate headquarters who would respond to the customers who were trying to contact me. I had a BlackBerry at the time, and as I responded to the corporate recruiter, they were reading everything I wrote. Given that they had recently laid off most of their workforce, I can't say I was misguided in trying to find another company to work for. It was just bad timing and poor judgment on my part.

When I finally returned to my home in Pennsylvania, I arrived shortly after a major storm had uprooted three massive oak trees in my back yard. There was not one piece of ground that was not covered by leaves, broken tree limbs, or fallen trees. It was a devastating mess that would take me weeks to clean up. Kind of like the years it would take to get my life back on track again.

Shortly before I left on my trip, I was contacted by a man I went to grade school and junior high with. He had just been released from prison and was trying to get in touch with people from his past. I was very lonely and vulnerable, so I befriended him, and he came to visit me a few times. Outside of my family, he was the only other person who came to my house in the woods.

We were never friends while in school, but I had tendency to talk with anyone. When he came to visit, we would sit on the couch and chat about life and his time in prison.

While I was traveling out west, he casually asked me what type of equipment I had at my house that was paid for. I had thousands of dollars' worth of lawn equipment, an ATV, and things I can't even remember. In my manic stage, I said, "I really don't need any of my things anymore." I don't know if he realized I was sick. But since I had shaved my head during one of my manic episodes and had deep, dark circles under my eyes, it would have been hard not to notice something wasn't quite right.

He went into my home and took almost everything. I know it was him because he told me. He said, "I opened a bank account, and I'll give you half of the money I made from selling your things." I never saw the money.

When I entered my house, it had been ransacked as if the same storm that had uprooted the trees had landed inside my house too. The only thing left was some Diet Pepsi in the refrigerator.

I never reported him to the police because I felt like it was my own fault. I had told him where I was traveling and how many hours it would take for me to get back home. I also didn't want to be responsible for him violating the terms of his parole. It doesn't make a lot of sense, but because I was involved in the legal system, I felt like I was a criminal too, and whatever happened to me, I deserved. Not clear thinking, but it was all I had to work with at the time.

After missing appointments with my doctor and therapist, I went back faithfully. I had called the office from Las Vegas and told them I was moving out west. They never said anything to me, and we continued my treatment as if I'd never missed a day. Neither of them asked me about why I was traveling out west or what I was thinking. My therapist told me I experienced a "dissociative fugue." I believe the real answer was I had a manic episode with a bit of psychosis. Both providers continued to miss the mark on what was wrong with me, and it's troublesome to look back and think had I been under the care of someone who treated me properly I might have been able to recover much sooner.

* * *

As my mental health continued to decline, so did my bank account. After my short-term disability was exhausted, the company I worked for gave me twelve weeks of unpaid medical leave. The day after the leave ended, I was fired. It took a few years, but little by little, I lost almost every material possession I owned. The first to go was my online-purchased RV. As much as I knew it was a whim to buy it, my dogs, Mom, and I had enjoyed traveling in it. It was the first domino in the chain reaction.

Eventually, I would lose my house, and that meant moving back to West Virginia with my mom or become homeless. I had been independent since I was eighteen years old and going to college in Tennessee. The idea of becoming dependent on Mom and my other family members was devastating.

After staying with Mom for several months, there was a knock at our front door. A man was standing at the door waiting to serve me with legal documents. The bank was notifying me they were foreclosing on my house. When he handed me the papers, a surge of anxiety flooded through my system. All I knew was I had to go back to the house and retrieve all my belongings.

The last time I walked out the door to my home, I felt completely defeated, as if I had lost the biggest game of my life. I went from having a winning record to ratcheting up a string of losses. Bipolar disorder was beating me. Even though I knew my loss was because of a mental illness and the fact I could not work, it made it even worse. I felt like I was on the bottom of a pile of a hundred people, and the pressure was making it difficult to breathe.

The mental toll of going from a successful businessperson with the lifestyle benefitting from a healthy income, to moving back home with my mom pushed me further into a place where I no longer wanted to live. I didn't know how I could ever face anyone outside of my immediate family. I would have to answer questions like, "How long have you been back in West Virginia?" "Where do you live?" "Where do you work?" I hadn't told anyone about my struggles with bipolar disorder, so my answers tended to be short and vague. But in the back of my mind, I always heard the tapes playing, "I have a mental illness. I had a mental health crisis and it completely disrupted my life." In some ways, it would have been more freeing to tell the truth, but I was not quite ready to disclose my illness to other people.

Fortunately, I hadn't posted tons of pictures on Facebook before my mental breakdown, making it a lot less obvious that my lifestyle had changed. What I learned from this more than humbling experience was it does not matter how many material possessions I have. If I don't have my health—physical or mental—I have nothing.

And more than just facing my financial challenges, I was dealing with the loss of close friendships. One of my saddest moments was realizing I went from being a person with lots of friends, a great deal of social interaction, and having fun activities, to a person who was completely isolated, with the exception of my immediate family. I lost touch with all my friends. It broke my heart to feel such loneliness. One of the hallmark signs of mental illness is isolation, and the more I isolated myself, the worse my mental health got.

If it hadn't been for Mom and Shelley, I can only imagine what would have happened to me. And as hard as it was on me to live through a very difficult time, it was painful for them to watch me deteriorate. I remember looking in the mirror at one point, not recognizing the face looking back at me. I was devastated at who I had become and hated myself because I believed I was completely responsible for what had happened. I carried mountains of guilt and oceans of blame with me for years.

Day after day was excruciatingly painful. I've had many broken bones from my days in sports, but I can say I had never experienced the kind of emotional pain I endured at the hands of my biggest competitor—bipolar disorder.

What really kept me going were my three dogs. No matter how long I slept, they stayed by my side. I would frequently move between the bed and the couch, and there they were, following me from room to room. There are actual service dogs for people with mental illness, and I firmly believe I had three deserving of the title.

We never had too many visitors at Mom's house, but my faithful Uncle Sam would stop in about twice a month. Sometimes I would get out of bed to talk with him, and other days I would close my door and go back to sleep.

Uncle Sam was sitting in the kitchen talking with my mother. I had gotten out of bed about noon. I said hello and went in the living room and sat on the couch with a blanket. Uncle Sam got up from the table and followed me into the living room.

He said, "How are you doing?"

"Just great. Every day is a party when you struggle with depression," I said in my most sarcastic voice.

He was standing a few feet from me and said, "You know, people do get better from depression."

"It doesn't matter," I said. "I've lost everything." I was beaten down and worn out from fighting to stay alive.

"Lots of people make it back, and you're going to be one of them."

I rolled my eyes as he walked out of the room. But in the end, he was right.

Chapter 15

Rebounding

After living in West Virginia for a few months, I ran into a woman whose daughter played AAU basketball. She suggested I go by the gym and watch one of her daughter's practices. The day I walked into the gym, I had no idea how much a bouncing basketball would impact me. I started helping out the team, and eventually I was asked to help coach at the high school I graduated from.

When I told one of the coaches I had bipolar disorder, he said, "Amy, the kids don't care what you have or what you don't. They just want someone to pay attention to them."

My high school basketball coach, Stanley Blankenship, welcomed me to the staff with open arms. He had been the girls' basketball coach for thirty years. When he asked me if I wanted to help coach, I was thrilled. It did not matter to him that I had a mental illness. He respected me for the person I was and did not judge me.

I spent one year going to all the practices and games. The young people were full of life and energy, and this helped my mood. I still had to fight depressive symptoms like lethargy and sleeping too much, but I was motivated every day to attend basketball practice. Some days it took a call from Coach Blankenship to get me out of bed, but I was always encouraged by the fact that he obviously cared for my well-being.

I also began researching mental health advocacy organizations. I was looking for a support group and eventually found the Depression and Bipolar Support Alliance (DBSA) in Wheeling, West Virginia. I wasn't sure what to expect the first time I went to a meeting. I simply knew I could not make the journey alone, and everything I read about peer support organizations reaffirmed that people who had been there could help me. The group was supportive, understood me, and they encouraged me to get well. There is something very powerful about peer support and knowing you are not alone.

The founder of DBSA in Wheeling encouraged me to participate in a group of people who were trying to recover from either depression or bipolar disorder. He had put together a special class utilizing the book *Pathways to Recovery: A Strengths Recovery Self-Help Workbook* by Priscilla Ridgway. It's a strengths-based approach to recovering, meaning a person focuses on his or her positive aspects and sets realistic goals, with the ultimate goal of regaining a life after a psychiatric diagnosis.

I found the class and the book extremely beneficial. There's something about someone pointing out how important my attitude was in my recovery process. All the things I once took for granted became huge milestones. I was accustomed to being the person doing the inspiring, and now I was the person who needed to be inspired by others in a big way. Over time, I've often looked back through my copy of *Pathways to Recovery*.

After the basketball season ended, I decided to try my hand in consulting work and landed a job with an old colleague. I worked for a few months, but then fell back into a deep depression when Chance, my dog who was with me for sixteen years of my life, had to be put to sleep. She had gotten to the point where she was blind and could barely walk any longer. I had hoped she would close her eyes gently and go to sleep, but as it turned out, I had to take her to the vet. It still breaks my heart.

My sister Sherry, who is a talented artist, created a beautiful oil painting of Chance and Shasta lying together in the grass. For the most part, when I look at the picture, I have many happy memories. But every now and then I get an empty pit in my stomach and wish dogs could live forever.

As part of my contracted role, I was writing a training manual on depression. Yet I still had not quite grasped the depth of what I was experiencing. Additionally, I had lost my confidence and self-esteem, given the position I was in. After eight months, I was forced to stop working again.

In the meantime, my other lab, Shasta, became very sick. Immediately after Chance died, she had begun to refuse to eat no matter what type of food I bought for her. Her health and demeanor changed rapidly after Chance was gone. They were best friends, and I wholeheartedly believe animals grieve, because I watched her do it. I took her to the vet, and he told me to keep her comfortable and bring her back when I was ready. About two weeks later, I took Shasta back to the vet. Losing another one of my best friends and beloved pets was as if someone was reaching inside of me ripping my heart out.

I continued to see Dr. Martin. I believe a part of me was too afraid not to be under the care of a psychiatrist, and I feared not being able to find another one. It's easy to look back and think about all the things I could've done differently, but that's hindsight. Decisions look much easier in the rearview mirror. The fact is, I don't know if a different doctor would have made any difference. I felt broken, and I'm not sure anyone can heal that feeling. Yet I have also learned how important it is to have a doctor who is helping a person make progress and not go backward.

When the consulting role was over, I retreated again in isolation for a few months until I got a phone call from a parent who wanted me to give her daughter basketball lessons. I'm not sure why I agreed to it, but I did, and I started training her once a week at the YMCA.

It was all I could do to drag myself out of bed to go work with Miranda, even though she always brought an eager attitude and a bright smile. Shortly after I began working with her, another parent called and, again, for whatever reason, I agreed to work with his daughter too.

For every two steps forward I took in healing, it seemed like I took three steps back. Coming out of my safe home to interact with other people meant I would have to begin facing the reality of where I was in my recovery journey. Dealing with my extreme weight gain, along with the added self-conscious vulnerability of not believing I was a good enough basketball trainer because I was not fit, weighed heavily on my mind. Every negative thought rolled into another, and soon it was a spiral down to darkness.

Before too long, I was sleeping well into the afternoon, and I began thinking about how I was going to take my own life. I cried so hard my eyes became puffy and swollen. I started to pray. I reasoned with God and said if only he would give me a horrible disease, I would not have to kill myself.

And then I started thinking about the kids whose lives I had touched and who had touched mine. I spoke out loud and said, "God, I hear you." In that moment, even if my life did not matter to me, I knew it mattered to those young girls who looked forward to basketball lessons, and so I agreed in my prayers to fight for just one more day.

Miranda and Josie never knew how much they meant to me. They were special in so many ways, but their presence in my life was the difference between life and death. After that day, I started fighting my suicidal thoughts with a vengeance, and eventually the thoughts subsided and the depression lifted. I started teaching more and more young people until I was working six days a week.

About a year into my basketball training business, I was asked to coach a boys' sixth-grade team. These boys had never met someone who expected them to run to every drill, hustle on the court, and try harder even when they didn't think they could. I believe because I raised the bar so high, they exceeded all expectations. I learned so much about myself from coaching those boys. I have to say it was one of the most rewarding things I have ever done.

As for results, we played about thirty games and went undefeated. Winning was great, but the biggest lesson came from a young boy, Sammie, who only got to play a few minutes in one game. It was a close game, and Sammie was not the most talented player on the team. This was only sixth-grade basketball, and though it was supposed to be about teaching the boys how to play the game, those of us who are competitive always want to win.

Sammie went missing when the game was over, and we found him crying under the bleachers. His parents met me the moment I picked up my clipboard. I tried to explain it was not intentional that I left Sammie out. The truth was I got caught up in winning the game. I apologized because I felt like I had made a mistake, and of course I felt badly Sammie was crying.

Then I had to remind myself that one of the many things participating in sports had taught me was that sometimes I was going to be disappointed. I was not always going to get my way. The question I found myself asking was, "Did I bounce back from the times when things got really tough?" Then the relevant question was, "How will Sammie respond in the next practice?"

This guy's fighting spirit truly made a mark in my mind. The next practice, he was diving on the floor for balls and finishing first in all the sprints. Sammie had responded in the way winners do. He got past his sadness and turned his energy in a positive way.

I took this lesson and applied it to my own life. It brought me back to a point in time that I had forgotten. I had been so consumed with bipolar disorder and all the turmoil caused by being ill that I didn't remember who I was. Sammie was the mirror I needed to turn my focus on the positive experiences in my life. When it comes to having grit, Sammie was the example who reminded me of myself.

By the time I stopped giving basketball lessons, I had worked with over two hundred kids. Each and every young person who I worked with will always hold a special place in my heart.

Chapter 16

The Cascade Begins

The worst thing to me about psychotropic medications is the weight gain. From the time I first started treatment with Dr. Martin, I gained a whopping eighty pounds. I'd lost about twenty pounds and really wanted to focus on getting back in shape, but despite spending anywhere from five to ten hours at the gym working with kids, I still couldn't lose any weight. I told Dr. Martin I was afraid of the physical effects like high blood pressure, high cholesterol, and diabetes. I suggested we stop one medication in particular that was known to cause significant weight gain. She agreed.

In September 2012, eight months after I'd stopped taking the medication, I began experiencing mania. I was sleeping for only a few hours a night, and I abruptly quit my basketball training business. I became paranoid and wasn't sure who I could trust.

Weeks passed like this, and I had an appointment with my doctor. I told her I was doing extremely well and that I had quit the basketball lessons and was moving on to other things. After my usual fifteen-minute appointment, she handed me a few prescriptions and said goodbye. She never asked me if I had been sleeping, lack of sleep being a key indicator for mania.

Four weeks later, I began having strange thoughts, like I knew something was wrong but I wasn't sure what to name it. I called my doctor's office and told the receptionist I needed to see Dr. Martin, but was informed the doctor was very busy and couldn't see me for another three weeks. I hung up the phone, not knowing what to do and not realizing what my other options were. I could have taken myself to the emergency room and asked to be admitted to the hospital, but my doctor couldn't provide a consult because she was an hour and a half away in another state. I could have called Dr.

Martin's office again and told them it was an emergency. I truly believed I only had a small window of time to acknowledge something was wrong before I would lose all insight into my condition. It was unfortunate the opportunity to get help passed.

Within a few days, I had a complete psychotic break. I thought my mom was trying to poison me and my dog, Buddy. I packed up a small bag with a change of clothes, put on my moccasin boots, and started driving west. I didn't know where I was going; I only knew I needed to get far away.

I drove all day and all night with Buddy in the back seat. I finally stopped at a hospital and went into the emergency room. It was as if I had a guardian angel on my shoulder looking out for me. But I couldn't articulate what was wrong. The hospital gave me a prescription for an acid reflux medication and discharged me. I never had a psychiatric evaluation.

I hit the road again, not realizing what direction I was traveling until I eventually ended up in a small town in Michigan on the border of Canada. It was a miracle I never crossed the border. I was driving northwest when I ran out of gas in the middle of the night.

I was exhausted, so I stayed with my truck until someone stopped to ask if I was okay. I told them to call an ambulance. I had been taking an anti-seizure medication for mood stabilization, and I abruptly stopped it, causing seizures. By the time the emergency squad arrived, I was having multiple seizures. My body was jerking, as if I were being shocked by a lightning bolt. The paramedics put me on a blanket on the ground and secured my neck. Eventually, they took me to a small community hospital to treat me. The only thing I said to the sheriff was, "Please take care of my dog, Buddy."

The sheriff contacted Mom, and she told him I had bipolar disorder and had stopped taking my medicine. Once I was stabilized, the sheriff told me they were sending me to another hospital in the city for additional tests. As soon as he said he had spoken to my mother, I had a fierce feeling of paranoia come over me. The same delusion about Mom poisoning me had returned. I began to have this internal racing thought dialogue.

"She's going to kill me. I don't know why she wants me dead. Everyone wants me dead. They all want to kill me. I'm scared. God, I am scared. Please help me. Please save me. I don't want to die."

On the outside, I was calm and relatively sedated from the medicine they'd given me, so I had no problem when they wheeled me out on a gurney and into the back of the ambulance. They didn't say where we were going or how long it would take to get there, but once the ambulance pulled away from the hospital, one of the emergency medical technicians pulled out a roll of adhesive tape, and the other held me down while they taped my arms and legs to the gurney. I asked why they were doing this, and one said it was because they didn't have restraints. I begged them not to restrain me with tape and told them I wouldn't give them any trouble.

To say I was traumatized would be an understatement. It scared me and set me off into an even worse state of mind. The drive was about two hours long, and by the time we arrived at an emergency room for psychiatric patients, I was completely out of touch with reality. And yet I remember when the social worker came into my hospital room.

"Are you Amy Gamble?" she asked.

"Yes." I was sure she was there to hurt me.

"Why are you here today? What's going on?"

I turned my head away from her, and a tear slid gently down my face. I did not know why I was there. I began to have another delusion that the hospital was an underground, black market place where they harvested victims' organs and sold them. I was terrified of everyone. My eyes were wide open, my gaze darting quickly around the room. I was plotting how I was going to escape.

"If you don't talk to me, I can't help you," she said with her frustration rising.

I thought, "I don't want your help, anyway."

She left the room. I lay there very still. I had an IV in my arm because they were giving me fluids to hydrate me. I don't think I had drunk any water for days and very little of anything else, so I was obviously dehydrated.

I slid my way off the bed with my bare feet hitting the cold floor. I pulled the IV out of my arm, and the blood started to squirt everywhere. I wiped it on my hospital gown. I crept to the doorway and saw all the hospital workers had their heads down writing in charts or talking on the phone. I knew it was time to make my escape.

I walked slowly past the desk, and no one noticed until I got to the exit. The emergency room I was in was a psychiatric E.R. They were accustomed to dealing with mental health patients, and they came running toward me like a herd of buffalo. I began to scream, "Let go of me." I don't remember all of what was said, but I know there was a "calm down" statement in there somewhere.

They took me back to the room and put me in bed. They all stood around my bed making sure I stayed in it. While they were putting the IV back in my arm, the bright hospital light blinded me. They must have given me a dose of a sedative because I was finally getting relief from the tormented thoughts in my mind. What was really humane was even though I had made quite a scene, they never used restraints. After all, I wasn't a wild animal. I was a human being in the throes of a brain gone awry.

After spending several hours in the emergency room, I was transported by another ambulance to a mental health hospital. This time the ambulance crew was respectful and very professional. They never used restraints and they put a blanket over me for the ride.

She said to me, "Ms. Gamble, we're taking you to another hospital where they're going to take care of you."

I answered, "Okay."

By the time we got to the hospital, it was late at night. The staff took me to my room, where I immediately went to sleep.

The next day I was taken back to the general hospital for tests. Because I'd had seizures, the doctors wanted to make sure I didn't have any brain damage. At the time, all they told me was that I'd be going back to the hospital. In my confused state, I wasn't sure what was going on. My delusional thoughts were saying everyone was trying to kill me, and the hospital wanted to harvest my organs. I was in pure terror, and the people who were trying to help me had no idea I didn't trust them.

I spent a few nights in the regular hospital with twenty-four-hour sitters by my side. Some people spoke to me, while others just stared like I was from another planet. I kept fairly quiet until a very kind hospital worker started to talk to me. She made me feel like a human being, and I trusted her. We talked about where I was from, and I asked her if I could use a computer because I wanted to get on Facebook.

What is so fascinating about psychosis is most people believe a person is not capable of retaining some reality. In my experiences, reality was this nebulous entity that came and went. One minute I could have a "normal" conversation, and the next minute I might be pacing the floor or running out the door, scared because my delusion was telling me a person was trying to hurt me.

My Facebook post had the number to the hospital and my room number "for people to call if they wanted." I mentioned I was having seizures. Fortunately, I don't think too many people saw my post, and only a few called. From my perspective, when I spoke to them, I was able to hold it together enough to not appear sick. No one knew I continued to think everyone was trying to kill me because I had a healthy heart and they wanted to sell it on the black market.

I was taken back to the mental health treatment facility. It was a large hospital with three separate wings. I took the medication they gave me for about three days. After that, I refused to take any medication because I thought it was poisoned. Psychiatric hospitals cannot forcibly treat patients. It's part of the patients' rights. When I was released after three weeks, I wasn't stabilized. I didn't have the right combination of medications, and the care seemed to be especially disorganized.

The psychiatrist who initially visited with me assured me they would get me out within a few days. He was the weekend psychiatrist.

The second psychiatrist I saw was sitting at a conference table with medical students lined up on each side. The treating physician was at the other end of the long table. I was intimidated with all the residents staring at me.

There were two residents who came to my room to personally talk with me. They knew I was an Olympian and had verified it by doing an online search. We talked about team handball and what my experience was like at the Olympics. This is one of the most intriguing parts of having psychosis—there are aspects of reality and even normalcy that can come through in interactions.

Small acts of kindness when a person is not well can go a long way and make a big difference. For some reason, I wasn't allowed to have my own shoes, and it was hard to walk through the hallways without them. I asked a staff member if she'd bring me a pair, and she did.

She was the one person on staff who said, "Amy, you are manic. You need to lie down and get some rest."

Hearing that statement kind of shocked me and made me question myself for a moment, thinking, "Is there something wrong with me?"

After a few nights, I stopped sleeping. I would look at my roommate and think she was working for the bad guys. I told myself I couldn't sleep because she would kill me. I had to stay awake. At night, they would mop all the floors, and I could smell the bleach-like cleaner. This triggered me and made me believe the hospital staff were killing people at night and using bleach to clean up the blood. One delusional thought rolled into another, and I was creating stories in my mind based on unreality.

There was one nurse who took a special liking to me. I think when I struck the chord of reality, I was a decent person and somewhat interesting to talk to. She was a basketball fan and had read that I had played at Tennessee. She thought that was pretty cool.

"What was it like to play for Pat Summitt?" she asked while sitting on the other bed in my room.

"She was an amazing coach. I learned lots of life lessons from her," I said with a sense of pride.

"That must have been really cool to be in the Olympics. What was that like?"

I launched into a story about opening ceremonies and what it was like to march into Olympic stadium. She listened, genuinely interested. For a moment, I would feel like a real person, and then time would pass and the delusions would return. None of the hospital staff knew I was experiencing delusions. I certainly was not going to tell them I thought they were trying to hurt me. But what did affect me was not having the right combination of medications, and the ones they gave me, I rarely took. The nice nurse who spoke to me with compassion and humanity always got me to take the medicine. There just weren't enough nurses like her.

I had no concept of what day it was, what year it was, or why I was in the hospital. But eventually Thanksgiving was approaching, and the doctor said it was time to release me.

Mom and Shelley drove to Michigan to pick me up. Shelley could tell I wasn't well and told the staff I needed longer treatment, but they disagreed with her. Besides, it was almost Thanksgiving, and they wanted to get people home for the holidays.

We picked up my truck that was being held at the local fire department garage, and Buddy was being kept at a doggy daycare. Shelley and I went in to get him, and I drove the entire way back to West Virginia.

As night approached, I would look in my rearview mirror and see headlights that had a blue tint. In my mind, I identified those lights as the cars that were following me. I never said anything about what I was thinking to Mom or Shelley. Shelley continued to watch me with this "I'm worried about you, and something isn't right" look, and I simply tried to discount it.

The thought in my mind was, "There is nothing wrong with me. Everyone else has the problem."

* * *

I stayed at home for five days, and then on December 1, 2012, I woke up around four in the morning, loaded my truck, and took off on the road again. My delusions were overpowering any chance for rational thinking. I drove southwest, stopping only for gas along the way. I'm not sure if I believed I would show up in Arizona on a friend's doorstep or not, but I never made it to Phoenix. I got to Albuquerque, New Mexico, and decided to stay at a hotel. At this point, I had driven over twenty-one hundred miles because I didn't take the fastest route to get there. I have no idea why, but I chose to go through Memphis, Tennessee, and that added over five hundred miles to the trip.

After checking into the hotel, I went to my room and took a shower. I suppose somewhere in my mind I knew I was not well. I took an anti-psychotic that Dr. Martin had given me several months prior, but any chance of getting stabilized vanished when a group of kids pounded on my door and scared me. I packed everything up, threw the remainder of my medications in the trash, and drove north to Denver.

Somewhere along the way, I think the medication I'd taken began working. I have always responded rapidly to medication. I thought if I could get to Denver, I'd get back on Interstate 70 and head home.

I made it safely to Denver, and then drove south to Colorado Springs. Feeling tired, I parked in a Walmart lot and went to sleep. I had now been awake for over two days. Very little sleep is needed during a manic period. It's like my body becomes a machine and the motor won't shut off. For people without a mental illness, sleep deprivation can cause psychosis. For someone who has bipolar disorder, it's a very dangerous situation.

Mom and the family knew I had been gone for a couple of days and had no idea where I was. But when I arrived in Colorado, I called her. There was a moment when I thought I would have someone in my family come get me, but that was a fleeting notion. I don't remember all of what I said, but I know I told Mom I was in Pennsylvania and not Colorado. I told her I would be home in a few days.

I spent two days in Colorado Springs, mostly driving around and taking an occasional hike. I visited the Garden of the Gods park and remember yelling about something that bothered me. I slept in my truck in the Walmart parking lot. I purchased a sweatshirt, which would later come in quite handy—probably even save my life.

After waking up one morning and thinking the world was coming to an end, I set out on the road again. I drove north through Wyoming, and then decided I would try to get to Las Vegas. Clearly, my thoughts were not rational. I also had very little money and no debit or credit cards. The only thing I had with me was a checkbook, and I learned I could write a check for twenty dollars over the amount of purchase at Walmart. I used the money for gas and, where retailers accepted them, I'd write a check. I am typically a very resourceful person who knows how to get things done. Even though I was psychotic, those skills didn't go away.

It was surprising I didn't run out of gas. Fortunately, my Chevrolet Avalanche had a thirty-gallon tank, and the electronic gauge let me know how many miles I had left before needing to refuel. I would get about twenty miles to the gallon, and so I'd only have to stop about once every six hundred miles.

Instead of going south to Utah, I went north to Montana. By the time I stopped in a small town west of Missoula, I had traveled another eleven hundred miles. I don't know what I was thinking when I took the exit and drove up a mountainside, but when I got to a log cabin, I believed the house was mine, and friends were waiting in the basement to give me a surprise birthday party.

The owners of the cabin weren't home. It was a beautiful two-story log cabin with a basement. The kitchen was spacious, and to my recollection, there were two bedrooms upstairs, a bathroom, and a sitting area. I checked around the house and found a side door that was open, so I went inside and made myself at home. There were items in a few of the bedrooms that I wanted to get rid of because I believed it was my house to do whatever I thought needed to be done to clean it up. I took all their picture frames off the dressers and threw them in the middle of the bed, breaking most of them. I made a fire in the potbelly stove, made some coffee, sat down, and watched television. I decided if I was going to stay there for the winter, I had better find a Walmart and get some supplies.

I got into the truck and drove back onto Interstate 90. By this time, my mind was racing so fast I couldn't keep up with the rapid-fire thoughts that were going through it. I continued driving all the way to the Idaho border in the middle of pouring down rain that turned to snow when I reached the mountains. Shortly after crossing the border, I took an exit for a national forest and proceeded to follow the snow-covered road.

I turned down a side road and began climbing up a steep hill. The snow was several inches deep, but the truck was four-wheel drive and able to trudge through. I finally made it to a part of the road that was fenced off with a little metal gate. For whatever reason, I drove through the gate and continued up the hill.

In my mind, people were in the truck with me. I was yelling at them, telling them to get out. I remember stopping the truck and screaming at the top of my lungs. It all felt so real, like someone was there yelling back at me. I had rarely ever experienced hallucinations before, but looking back, that was terribly real.

The snow got deeper, more than a foot, and the truck finally came to a stop after I ran over a large tree that had fallen in the road. It never even fazed me that I was stuck in the snow, on the side of a mountain, and with no way to call for help.

Instead, I got out and started hiking in more than a foot of snow. I was wearing a pair of nylon sweatpants, a nylon shirt, sweatshirt, and a pair of moccasin boots without socks—not dressed for the elements I was about to encounter.

I continued following the path until I came upon a warming hut in the middle of the woods. It was completely dark, but I could make out the outline of a potbelly stove. The hut was filled with piles of newspapers and stacks of wood. These structures were primarily used by snowmobilers in the winter to warm themselves between rides. I made a fire in the stove and lay down on the dirt floor beside it, where I fell asleep for the first time in days.

When I woke up, I was freezing. I was shivering so much my teeth chattered. I tried to put more wood on the fire, but it wouldn't stay lit, so I took a pile of papers and started a fire outside the door in between almost six feet of highly banked snow.

Quite a bit of time passed, and I turned away from the hut and began walking back the way I had come. When I got to my truck, I saw one of the tires was destroyed from running over the tree. I opened the door and took out a travel portfolio containing my checkbook and driver's license. I locked the door and continued down the mountain.

As I walked, the snow started to fall, covering my footsteps. It was pitch black, and I could only see two feet ahead of me as I made my way deeper and deeper into the sea of trees in the middle of the national forest.

Chapter 17

Lost and Found in the Wilderness

It was night by the time I'd wandered my way around the mountainside and down what I later learned was a dirt road. I thought if I went down to the stream, I might find a forest ranger's office. But when the sun came up, I was spiraling into a web of mental confusion. I had been an avid hiker and backpacker for years, and I had some natural survival skills, and my instincts were telling me to keep moving because if I stopped I would freeze to death.

I walked all the way down to the bottom of the ravine. I didn't find a forest ranger's office, but I did find a large stream. I don't know why, but I turned around and began walking back up the mountain. When I got fairly high up, I could see my deep tracks in the snow were still there. I was so tired that I lay down under a few large pine trees where I made a bed and went to sleep. I woke up when rain started pouring down.

The sweatshirt I was wearing was soaked from the rain, but my nylon shirt underneath was providing some protection. My toes were so numb I could no longer feel them. I got back off the path and started walking down the dirt road again. It was like I was stuck in a mental loop, walking miles up the road, and then miles back down the road.

At first, I didn't know I was in any danger, but then I realized I was sick. It was as if someone was flipping a switch in my brain from madness to harsh reality. I have this vivid memory of hiking back up the mountain and suddenly praying, "Dear God, I am mentally ill. Please forgive me and help me. Please help me make it home safe." Each time I lay down to rest, I prayed to God to forgive me for putting my life in danger because I thought I wasn't going to wake up again.

By the time it was daylight again, I would rest periodically then get this sudden jolt that felt like an electrical shock. I forced myself to get back up and start moving again. When I realized I was lost, I was afraid. The only thing that kept me going was saying my prayers. As the day passed and night came again, I knew the only way to stay alive was to keep walking.

By the third morning, my clothes were drenched, exposing my skin to the freezing weather. My legs were chafed, and large sores slowed my walking pace. My boots were soaking wet, leaving my feet feeling like a hundred pounds of lead. I could no longer feel the ground underneath me.

To make matters worse, I decided to cross the stream. I thought if I could get to the other side, I might find some people. That meant walking in water just below my knees, which is about two feet. I carefully measured every step so I wouldn't fall. I found a gigantic stick that I used to measure how deep the water was, staying away from the deeper parts. I crossed the stream four times and I never fell, though at one point I considered lying down and letting the water take me to civilization. Thank God I didn't listen to that thought.

After crossing the stream, I climbed up the side of a mountain to try to find a way out. But all I could see were hundred-foot-tall evergreen treetops. Total despair came over me. I'd been out in the forest for three days, and I hadn't had anything to drink. I was so thirsty after walking for miles. Using my hands as a cup, I drank water from the ice-cold stream, refreshing my thirst but freezing my hands. It was one of the few times I had taken my hands out of my sweatshirt. Even in my mixed-up state, I still had the wherewithal to know I had to protect my extremities from the elements.

Since I couldn't see anything but trees, I tried to retrace my steps back through the forest in my desperate search for civilization. At times, I would see what looked like smoke coming from a fireplace, and then I realized it wasn't real.

I followed the running water flowing down the side of the mountain into the bigger stream. At one point, I took a large stick and used it for leverage to keep myself upright. It was working out well until I slipped and fell. The end of the stick drove into my numb right leg, tearing my pants and making a gash four inches long. It hurt, but I kept walking anyway.

Evening was coming, and the temperature was dropping again. Sadness swept over me. I knew deep in my heart that my only chance of survival was if someone rescued me.

Facing a near-death experience did something very powerful to my psyche. I can't say I was completely mentally healthy, but it jolted me back into reality and kick-started my will to live.

I kept talking out loud, saying, "Keep walking, keep walking," and I sang a few songs to keep my mind occupied. I was walking like Frankenstein because my feet were so numb.

As I stumbled along, I heard a noise in the distance that sounded like ATVs. I tried to run to them, but it was impossible because of my numb legs and frostbitten feet. At first, the sound of the engines was quite loud, and then suddenly, it was quiet. I walked as fast as I could in the direction of the sound, and finally I saw two people, a man and a woman, who instantly became my heroes.

I startled the woman when I approached them. People out on ATVs aren't likely to run into someone else that deep in the forest. Not many people hike such places in the middle of the winter, and hunting season was over.

"What's your name? Are you alone?" she asked.

"Amy Gamble," I said, staring into her eyes. "I'm alone."

"What are you doing in the middle of the forest all alone?" she asked as she gently put both her hands on my cheeks.

"I got lost. I was on a hike." That was the only thing I knew to say.

The man said, "Let's build a fire and get her warm."

She said, "I don't think we should build a fire. We should just get her out of here." She turned to me and asked, "Where is your car?"

"I don't know. Somewhere in the mountains."

"We'll give you a ride out of here, but when we get to our car, we're going to have to call the sheriff. Do you understand?"

"Yes. That's okay," I said eagerly. "I need help."

Her eyes were shocked, but incredibly kind, and she knew something was wrong with me. She said she was a respiratory therapist and told me her and her brother's names. I wish I could remember them.

The man gave me a heavy jacket and covered my legs with a plastic emergency blanket. She told me he would ride me out of the forest, and she would follow. The ride seemed to last forever, and it was so cold I felt like I was sitting in a giant-size freezer with a huge fan blowing on me.

We finally arrived at the parking area where their truck and trailer were parked. They turned on the truck heater and insisted I take off my wet clothes, and they called for the sheriff and the paramedics. I sat in the front seat of a stranger's truck, shivering, teeth chattering, stark naked, and vomiting out the door. Apparently, the water from the stream made me deathly ill. Of course, I had no water purifier with me.

When the sheriff asked where my vehicle was, I told him somewhere in the mountains. I had no idea where I was in relation to where I entered the forest. To this day, I still don't know where they found my truck. He asked if there was anyone he could call for me, and I told him no. Then he let the paramedics help me, and they transported me to a hospital in Coeur d'Alene, Idaho.

The hospital emergency room staff was very compassionate. However, everyone seemed convinced I had tried to take my own life. They kept asking me if something happened to make me want to die. I kept explaining to them that I had gotten lost.

As the warmth began to thaw my frostbitten feet, I cried out. The process of rewarming frozen tissue is excruciating. Outside of extreme emotional pain, I can't say I have experienced anything as agonizing as frostbitten feet warming up. After a few hours in the emergency room, I was admitted to the hospital for dehydration and frostbite.

The first nurse I had could not have been nicer. She had light brown hair, and was physically fit and rather tall. She and an aide piled pillows behind me and propped up my feet. They were giving me pain medicine for the frostbite, and whenever the medication machine buzzed because the line had tangled, she was there to fix it. I was awake most of the night, and the longer I stayed up, the more delusional I became. The same delusions about people wanting to kill me had returned, and some of the staff did not do much to earn my trust.

After the night shift, I had a nurse from hell. She was rude, mocked me, and turned my pain medication machine off. She was thin, had dark hair, and wore glasses. I wasn't intimidated by her, but I thought she was evil. I needed the medicine to bear the pain from the circulation returning to my frozen feet, but she didn't think I needed it, so she unplugged the machine and moved it to the other side of the room.

Additionally, there was a student nurse who was learning how to insert IVs, and I thought she was on a gold-digging expedition in my arm trying to find a vein. I was dehydrated, so it was even more difficult, but she caused me so much pain, silent tears were rolling down my face. Finally, the nurse who had taken such good care of me earlier told her to stop and sent her out of my room. I thought she was an angel, and perhaps she was.

There were many doctors who came to see me during the day. I can't remember all the specialties except for the wound care doctor and the psychiatrist. My legs were badly burned from my wet, cold pants chafing them, creating wounds on the inside of my thighs. And, of course, my toes were mildly frostbitten, except for my right little toe that was black where the damage was more severe. They told me I was lucky I didn't lose it. The treatment for the frostbite was two weeks of injections of Heparin in my stomach to help the circulation improve. The only permanent damage I ended up with was a large scar on one of my toes. It was a miracle my injuries weren't more severe.

The primary care doctor called for a psychiatric consultation. The psychiatrist who came asked me a few questions in a non-threatening way. I trusted her, and I'm not sure why, but this relationship with her would prove extraordinarily important in my road to recovery. During our conversation, I told her I had previously been diagnosed with bipolar disorder and post-traumatic stress disorder. She listened, took notes, and asked me if I would agree to treatment. I said yes. Then she told me I would need a shower before coming to the psychiatric unit. It'd been about a week since I had taken a shower, and my hair smelled like burnt wood and was tangled like a bug caught in a spider's web.

The physical therapist who came to help me said the wounds on my legs were too raw, so instead of getting into the shower, I was given dry shampoo. It would be a few more days until I actually stepped into running water.

As the hospital worker wheeled me out of the overflow hospital room, the evil nurse stood at the nurses' station and laughed. I said, "Goodbye," and waved to all the nurses.

And she replied, "Have a great trip, Loo-Loo."

I sat quietly in the wheelchair as we made our way to the psych unit.

Chapter 18

Getting on the Right Road

The population of Coeur d'Alene, Idaho, is just over 45,000, which meant the behavioral health unit was not that large. I was fortunate they had a bed for me. This is also the town the late actress and bipolar advocate Patty Duke made her home. The hospital staff made a point of telling me about her, but I knew this from reading Duke's book, *A Brilliant Madness: Living with Manic-Depressive Illness*, several years earlier.

After I was moved to the psych unit, my stress level triggered my delusions, and I thought everyone was trying to kill me. For some reason, I felt compelled to tell the staff what I was thinking, and this made all the difference in the world in how long they kept me in the hospital and what type of medications I was given.

Dr. Carson, who had wavy brown hair and stood six feet tall, said, "You think I want to harvest your organs? I don't need your organs." She laughed, and I just looked at her. For the first time, I was challenged to question my delusional thoughts.

Questioning a delusion was like asking a question, and then saying *real* or *not real*.

They want to kill me. No, they don't. That's a delusion. They want to help me.

Then I would ask the staff a question for affirmation. "Do you want to help me?"

One major difference in my stay in Idaho from my stay in Michigan was that I was very compliant with the medications. It was so much better for me and the staff because I was more than willing to do what they suggested. And I'm among the fortunate who respond well to medications.

After a week in the hospital, Dr. Carson walked into my hospital room with a troubled look on her face. She said, "I just got off the phone with your mother. Your family wanted me to tell you…your dog Buddy was hit by a car."

I felt the tears welling up in my eyes. I started to shake and cry. I immediately blamed myself because I had been sick and unable to care for him.

She said, "It's not your fault. You gave Buddy a good life. One he probably would never have had without you." All I did was shake my head and cry as Dr. Carson patted me on the shoulder.

With Chance, Shasta, and Buddy all gone, it also closed a chapter in my book that was tied to Arizona. I hadn't just lost my dogs, I had lost my best friends. They were my family. We had made so many memories together, and often it was just me living life with my dogs and no human friends. I truly believe those dogs are the reason I am even writing these words. There is no love like the unconditional, loyal love of a dog.

* * *

Prior to ending up in the Idaho hospital, I had been treated at seven other facilities around the country—some very prominent facilities—but the care I received in Idaho was by far the best. Not only was the staff respectful, they were also extremely caring.

Shirley, a psychiatric nurse with twenty-one years' experience, took the time to give an hour-long formal presentation about bipolar disorder. She said, "You have a brain disorder and *it is not your fault. When you're ill, you can't believe your brain.*" She continued, "Start from where you are and learn as much as you can." It was the best advice anyone had given me, and it made such a tremendous impact I wrote it down. In fact, I wrote almost everything down. Once I had become stable, I used writing as a tool to help me heal.

It was the first time anyone had put bipolar disorder in those terms for me. She explained the biology and how our brains function. She talked about the signs and symptoms of mania and depression. There was a group of us, along with a few family members, and we were encouraged to ask questions. I don't remember everything, but what I do remember changed how I look at myself and my illness. Even though how I ended up in Idaho was a real tragedy, it turned out to be a place that would change the course of my life and start the long recovery process I would endure.

I spent my forty-eighth birthday in the psych unit. People wished me a happy birthday, and Mom, Shelley, and a friend from Philadelphia called to do the same. If I had to spend my birthday in the hospital, I could not have picked a safer place.

During this time, the Sandy Hook Elementary School shooting occurred. The patients and staff felt sorrow for the loss of all those innocent children, and the impact of such a horrendous crime can do more damage to the stigma of living with a mental illness.

People with mental illness are more likely to be the victim of violent crimes than perpetrate them. However, when something so horrific happens and the person is shown to have a mental illness, as was the case with the Sandy Hook shooter, it perpetuates fear and misunderstanding in the public's perception of all of us who live with a mental illness. It makes people with mental illness not want others to know for fear they may be labeled violent as well. It is true that some people with mental illness have violent outbursts and sometimes tragic outcomes occur. But those are the exceptions, not the majority.

* * *

Christmas came a week later, and one of the nurses asked if I'd like anything special to eat or drink. I asked for Starbucks coffee, and she said she'd bring some tomorrow. Christmas Day in the psych ward was pleasant because of the kind and compassionate people who sincerely cared about their patients.

The hospital required the patients to wear street clothes during the day. I had a couple of things from the donated clothes closet, and Mom sent me a package with a pair of shoes, jeans, and a t-shirt. My friend Julie from Philadelphia sent me a couple pairs of socks and a sweatshirt. Whenever we were allowed to go outside, I wore a winter coat from the clothes closet. It never even entered my mind that there was anything significant about using donated clothes. I had been taken back to a place where the only thing that mattered was my survival, and whatever I needed to do was what mattered most.

In the nightstand by my bed I found a blue copy of the New Testament, and I read it every day. I might not have trusted people, but I still trusted God. My mother had given me a beautiful gift when she took me to Sunday school. Over the years, I developed a spiritual relationship with God and found comfort in prayer, especially in my most vulnerable moments.

Meanwhile, the hospital had received a phone call from a sheriff in Montana who had found an identification tag that had my name and phone number on it. It was found outside the house I had entered. They had determined where I was from by the area code and phone number and tracked down Mom to find out where I was. She told them I was in a hospital in Idaho. When I called her, she'd wanted to know what I had done to have a sheriff in Montana looking for me.

The social worker in the hospital kept checking the listing to see if I had a warrant for my arrest, but continued to tell me everything was okay and everyone understood I was sick. She was reassuring, but I was not so convinced.

After three weeks of hospitalization, I was released. I could have benefitted from a longer stay, but compared to my average stays of forty-eight hours, three weeks was an eternity.

One of the criteria for being released was that I have somewhere to go. I was given a resource list of various places that might accommodate me. I called a bed and breakfast that housed family members when their loved ones were receiving treatment for cancer. I explained my situation, and they agreed to let me stay there until I could find somewhere else to go.

At this point, I had convinced myself I needed treatment from this facility in Coeur d'Alene, and the only way to get that treatment was to move to Idaho. My thinking had not completely cleared. It was impractical to believe I was moving to another city, clear across the country, with literally the shirt on my back. I know it's possible; it just wasn't rational.

The authorities were able to locate my truck. It was at an impound lot with a six-thousand-dollar towing charge for removing it from the side of the mountain and a one hundred and fifty dollars per day fee for storage. I had racked up a significant amount of financial obligations in the course of two months.

When I arrived at the bed and breakfast, the ladies there could not have been nicer. They knew I was coming from the psychiatric ward, and never once did they treat me with anything but kindness and respect. Both women were in their late sixties and very sweet. One was a little heavy-set with light brown hair and loved to give everyone hugs. The other woman was tall and slender. Her family had some struggles with mental illness, and she told me, "You don't have to be ashamed of this."

The bed and breakfast was in a large old house that was donated by a very wealthy family. There were about ten rooms, set up like a typical hotel room—shower, two beds, and a television. But there were also a community living room and kitchen.

During the day, I would get up, sit at the kitchen table talking to one of the ladies, and then go out walking. One of my favorite places to go was a local bagel shop. I wrote a check for twenty dollars and one of the women cashed it for me, giving me enough money to buy a Starbucks coffee and a bagel for a couple of days.

I filled my prescriptions and bought canned goods and Diet Coke at the local Rite Aid store. They accepted my checks without a problem.

It was December, so it was snowy and cold. The town sits at the base of a mountain range and is absolutely gorgeous. Broadcaster Barbara Walters called Coeur d'Alene "a little slice of heaven," and included it in her list of the most fascinating places to visit. It's no wonder I wanted to move there.

After a few days out of the hospital, I designed a plan to get an apartment. I found several places that were within walking distance of the hospital. The one problem was I had lost my driver's license in the forest. One of the ladies offered to give me a ride to the driver's license office, but I wanted to walk and take in all the sights. I had Mom send me my birth certificate, a checkbook, and some other forms of identification. When I pulled my things out of the bag on the counter, the lady at the DMV gave a look of exasperation. I can only imagine what she must have been thinking.

As the woman searched through the computer, she looked at me rather strangely, but then she told me to go to one of the computers and take the driving test. When I'd finished the test, I returned to the counter and was met by a sheriff, who came and stood inches from me.

I turned to the woman behind the counter and said, "I passed your test."

She replied, "You can come back another time and get your license."

The sheriff asked me my name and told me to walk outside. Once outside, he pulled my hands behind my back, put me in cuffs, and arrested me.

He said, "You know what you did, don't you?"

I was silent.

I sat without saying a word in the back of the cruiser. My head was down and my mind racing. I had an idea of what I had done while psychotic, and now I wondered what was going to happen to me.

When we got to the jail, the sheriff radioed in that he had arrived with the suspect and that she was "cooperative." Can't imagine what would have happened if I was not. I gave my bag of belongings to an officer, was searched, and then led to a holding area to wait until my name was called for intake.

I was able to use a phone, and I called Mom. "I need you to listen to me because I don't have much time to talk. I'm in jail in Coeur d'Alene. Please find me an attorney and get me out of here."

Mom was in shock but she listened intently. The last several weeks, I had put her and my closest family members through a living hell. She worried constantly about me and only wanted to bring me home safely. I have no words for how grateful I am to Mom for her support and steadfast faith that everything was going to work out all right.

My turn finally came for the intake. I was being arrested for illegally entering the log cabin, breaking and entering, and destruction of property. I was also being charged with arson because I had built an outdoor fire in the back yard of the home.

They asked me several questions, and one was whether I had a mental illness. I told them I was recently released from a psychiatric hospital. Fortunately, I had gone to the pharmacy and filled my prescriptions when I was released. They took down the name of the pharmacy to verify I had done what I said, then they put me in a holding cell. It had a bed with a blanket, a stainless steel toilet, and a sink. There was no room to pace the floor, and my anxiety was boiling to the top of my head. All I could do was curl up in a ball on the bed.

At one point, I heard a woman's voice through the cell door. I told her I needed my medicine and that I would like to be placed with other people. I don't think a person gets many choices while in custody, yet it never hurts to ask.

Mom called the ladies where I was staying and asked them to bring my medications to the jail. Apparently, if the jail stocked the medication I was taking, they would give it to me, but if not, I couldn't get it unless someone brought me my own prescription. The manager of the bed and breakfast, who I'd met only once and talked to for a few minutes, took the time to bring my prescriptions to the jail. It was an amazing act of goodness, and I am overwhelmingly touched by what she did for me.

A few hours passed, and I was moved to a larger holding cell with other women who were waiting to be assigned to a long-term cellblock. Wearing only an orange jumpsuit, I was constantly freezing. One of the women learned a trick to keep the heat on continuously, and she periodically did so. There was a metal temperature gauge on the wall, and she had discovered if she put a piece of cold, wet toilet paper on the metal gauge it would kick on the heat. I was thrilled every time she did it.

It's hard to forget a night in jail, let alone being incarcerated on New Year's Eve. When I went to sleep on a top bunk, the cell was mostly empty. By the middle of the night, there were women sleeping on the floor because there were no more beds remaining. Most people were arrested for either DUI or public intoxication.

I remember a very young girl who was crying and terrified. She was a college student who had been home for Christmas break and attended a New Year's Eve party. She was arrested for DUI. The next morning while we ate breakfast, I convinced her to reach out and call her father. She was terrified he would be angry with her. By the end of the day, her dad came and bailed her out.

After two nights in the temporary holding cell, I was moved to a different section of the jail, where some women had been held for a year or two. The very idea of spending years in jail or prison terrified me. Was this going to be my fate?

Chapter 19

Shock Sets In

For the most part, the women in the cellblock were easy to get along with. Almost everyone was there as a consequence of drugs, alcohol, mental illness, or some combination of the three.

A woman I'll call Leah, who was in her mid-forties with light brown hair and of average height and weight, shared her story that made me want to cry. She was a soccer mom with three kids from a middle-class neighborhood. Her husband worked in retail, and they had been married for quite some time. She was well known in her community as a fundraiser, and she led a massive project building a new outdoor sports complex.

Leah told me she'd found out her husband was having an affair with a woman he worked with. In order to cope with her broken heart, she turned to alcohol. While drunk, she called the store where her husband worked and threatened to blow them up with a bomb. She was arrested shortly after that.

Her upstanding reputation in the community was ruined, and so was her marriage. When she was released from jail the first time, she was not permitted to drink any alcohol. She'd violated that agreement and was now back in jail. One of the terms of her release was that she had to have a home to go to, but she had since become homeless.

But Leah was a woman of great faith. Every night, she led a group of women in prayer. In fact, she personally prayed for me that everything would work out and I would be given the break she felt I deserved. Leah made the time I spent in the Idaho jail more tolerable.

After a few days, I was sent before a judge. The corrections officers explained to me that I needed to agree to be extradited back to Montana. I was overwhelmed. I didn't understand the terminology and what was going to happen to me. Essentially, I did what they suggested.

What's most abundant in jail is time—to read, think, sleep, watch television, play cards, and pace the floor. If I had family or friends who wanted to visit me, I wouldn't have been able to physically see them. Visitation was done with a system very similar to video conferencing. When a visit was scheduled, the person would dial into the phone on the wall that had a screen. It was like using FaceTime.

I continued having a hard time getting warm. My bottom bunk was up against the outside wall, and it was freezing. One woman who was leaving gave me a white t-shirt she had purchased through the commissary. She told me to pay it forward when I left and give it to someone else. Wearing the cotton t-shirt under my orange jumpsuit made me much more comfortable. It also allowed me to hold onto being human by finding small things that brought me emotional comfort or some type of pleasure, something that is hard to do when sitting in a jail cell.

When I arrived on the cellblock, the television was turned off. I later found out that it was a disciplinary action because someone had done something the guards did not approve of. I don't know what they did, but I soon learned that manipulating the heat was a sure way to end up in isolation and lose commissary privileges. I had no money in the commissary account and wasn't going to be there long enough to buy anything, but when the other ladies got their commissary bags delivered, it was like Christmas. I wouldn't say it was a magical experience; however, it did lift people's spirits. One of my bunkmates shared a piece of cinnamon Jolly Rancher with me. I have never tasted anything so good.

* * *

Driving back to the small town in Montana where I had illegally entered someone's home would have normally taken two hours. Instead, it took all day. Riding in a van with your hands and legs cuffed is not very comfortable. But, unknowingly, I had broken the law, and I now found myself at the mercy of the system and in a heap of trouble.

One of the things Leah told me at the jail in Idaho was to not be afraid of the small-town jail. She said people in small towns are usually very nice and to not let my imagination about how horrible it was going to be run away from me. It was advice I needed to hear, and it helped me to remain calm and eliminate unnecessary anxiety, because there was plenty of needed anxiety to run on for years.

It was late afternoon when the van pulled into the Montana jail. I hadn't noticed the countryside during my manic and psychotic episode to appreciate the beauty and, had it not been under terrible circumstances, I would have marveled at the scenery. In fact, during our drive, I saw a moose drinking water at one of the streams. It wasn't my first time in Montana; I'd been there several years prior on a backpacking trip, and I knew it was beautiful country. Even in my dire circumstances, I could still appreciate that.

As Leah had said, the folks in the Montana jail were very courteous. The officer had me sit on a bench and proceeded to prepare the fingerprinting machine. If I had the technology to beam myself to another planet, I would have. I stood there numb while I was fingerprinted and photographed. Not in a million years did I ever believe anything like this would happen to me.

After I was "checked in," the officer led me down a hallway to a cellblock big enough for four people. Since I had come from the fairly large jail in Idaho, this place seemed extraordinarily small. When he locked the door behind me, I didn't know how I was going to survive for however long I had to stay. I knew it was going to take another miracle to get me out of the mess I'd created because of my untreated mental illness.

The one thing I was allowed to bring with me into the cell was my little blue Bible I'd gotten from the hospital. While in jail, I spent time reading, writing, and watching women's college basketball. I wrote a prayer that I have said multiple times in the past several years.

Dear God,

Please help me in my recovery. Lead me to the right paths so I may take my life back again. Give me strength to face seen and unforeseen challenges and adversity. Help me see all the gifts and blessings before me. Allow me to once again use my skills and talents in a productive way. Thank you, God, for all my miracles.

As far as my mental health, I continued to receive my medications twice a day. The staff even called the hospital in Idaho to have my prescription renewed for me.

The reality is, no matter what situation I have found myself in, I always manage to find the best and quickest way to deal with it. After around two weeks in jail, I became a trustee. I prepared the food trays for everyone and washed the dishes afterward. I also washed all the jumpsuits and bedding. This meant I would be out of my cell during the time I worked, and that was enough to help me feel like an individual and not an animal locked in a cage. Without conscious awareness, I was enlisting healthy coping strategies.

It also gave me the opportunity to talk with a corrections officer. He was a friendly older man in his late fifties who worked a few days a week. He let me out of my cell and checked on me in the kitchen as I prepared the meals. He was very professional, but the one thing he said I will never forget is, "Amy, we don't look at you like a criminal. We know you were mentally ill when this happened. It will all work out; just be patient."

The saving grace was the opportunity to call Mom once a day from the pay phone. I was able to write a check to the jail, and they would put money on my "books." The phone calls were extremely expensive, but hearing her voice always made me feel human. Instead of wanting to move to Idaho, I had been jolted back to reality. All I wanted to do now was go home to the hills of West Virginia and see my family. I envisioned myself sitting in a chair in the back yard, drinking a cup of Starbucks coffee and feeling the breeze brush across my cheek. This powerful imagery gave me the strength to deal with the pressure of being in jail and not knowing what my future held.

I was in jail a few days before an attorney came to see me. He knew I had bipolar disorder. Somehow, my story was traveling ahead of me. He was kind and completely understood mental illness, as his father-in-law had bipolar disorder.

As he asked me questions, he made a joke I didn't understand, to which I replied, "I have a mental illness, but it doesn't make me stupid." He quickly apologized for the misunderstanding.

Fortunately, most of the time, I had my own individual cell inside the small cellblock. During one weekend, there were four of us in the small space, and I think I was more relieved than they were when they were released.

Every now and then we were permitted to go to a larger room to exercise. Exercise consisted of pacing back and forth in the limited space. After a few times of this, I opted to stay in my cell and read.

Jan, my cellmate, had been in jail for several weeks. She had long, dark brown, greasy hair and stood about 5'9". In the three weeks I was in jail with her, she might have taken two showers. The shower was in the main area of the tiny cellblock, so it was noticeable when the water was running and when it was not.

It was never clear to me what had happened, but it was evident she was having some mental health challenges. She had a stack of legal books and a mountain of papers with which she was working on her own case. At that point, she had refused an attorney and wanted to represent herself.

There were no problems until the day she had a fit and threw the papers all over the small cell. I talked to her calmly and suggested she pick up the papers. She looked at me with big, brown, wild eyes and then began to calm down. I started picking up the papers, and she joined in and helped me.

We never talked very much, and after her minor explosion, nothing else happened until the day she passed out on the floor in the cell. Apparently, they had changed her medication, and she had been complaining it made her dizzy for a few days. I was sitting on my bed reading when I heard all the commotion.

When I approached her on the cell floor, I asked, "Are you okay?" She moaned. I went to the wall and pressed the call button for the guards.

"What do you need?" the woman said.

"My cellmate fell, and she's hurt."

They sent a corrections officer right away, and within hours they took her to a doctor in town.

One day Jan had a screaming fit. The corrections officer had come and told her she was going to have a mental health evaluation. She yelled, screamed, and protested. But the day before, she had gone to court and cussed out the judge and prosecutor, prompting the evaluation.

I told her, "I would consider the mental health evaluation a blessing." In the back of my mind, I thought, "Come on. They did you a favor."

To keep track of time, I took a piece of paper and made my own personal calendar. I started to become well enough mentally that I could backtrack where I had been and remember what had happened. Surprisingly, even though I had been experiencing psychosis, it did not have much effect on my memory. In some ways, I believe that is one of the cruelest things about bipolar disorder for me—remembering all the crazy stuff I did while I was sick, and then having to process and deal with it.

I was interviewed by a psychologist and told her about my delusions. She gave me a test to determine whether I was telling the truth. I told her I wished it was all a bad dream. She went to great lengths to obtain my medical records. I had written down on her form all the places I had treatment, including Dr. Martin. I know Dr. Martin was interviewed because she wrote me a letter firing me as a patient because I had been incarcerated.

The day came I was to appear before the judge. The friendly corrections officer led me up the stairs. When we got to a view of the outside doorway, he said, "I hope you're not planning on running anywhere, 'cause you won't get too far."

"Hadn't planned on it," I replied with a smile.

I shuffled into the courtroom with chained legs and arms, and I felt sick to my stomach. The charges against me were very serious and, if convicted, I would spend years behind bars. But my attorney assured me he was working with the prosecutor to come up with an agreement. I was later given a psychological evaluation, and my medical records were reviewed by the contracted psychologist.

The court determined I was mentally incompetent during the time I entered the house. My undertreated mental illness had caused great pain to people who did not even know me. It was not fair to them that I had crossed their paths. Never in a million years would this have happened if I had not been living with an undertreated mental illness. I feel like a victim of the system on one hand, and fully accountable on the other. It's very difficult to accept "what is" when I know I was not the only person responsible for what happened. But in order to move forward with my life, I had to let go of the past and not worry about who I should be blaming for some of the circumstances I found myself in.

For the most part, jail was miserable. The food, according to my journal entry, was "crappy." Friday night was peanut butter sandwiches on white bread with milk. My favorite was hotdog day, and once I even had two because Jan didn't eat hers. The highlight was being able to buy some snack food and Folgers instant coffee. I am a huge coffee drinker, and when the Folgers instant coffee touched my lips, I felt a sense of joy and peace. It was the small pleasures that kept me going.

My attorney was true to his word, and within three weeks I was released to the custody of Shelley, who'd flown across country to get me. I am not sure what I would have done without her. Mom's health was not the greatest, and no one else, with the exception of three other family members, knew what had happened. Shelley was my only hope, and she came through in a big way.

The first thing Shelley did was take me to get something to eat. I drank my first real cup of coffee in three weeks and savored every minute of it. It might be hard to understand how I could find so much enjoyment from a cup of coffee, but I had learned from many years of traveling through adversity that focusing on the little things can be the difference between surviving and wanting to give up.

While we were driving back to Idaho, we passed by the forest where I had gotten lost. Viewing it from a sane perspective made me acknowledge what a true miracle it was that I had been rescued. I still don't know if I truly grasped the significance of what I experienced. It would take years to heal all the wounds. Sometimes I still feel like I was in a movie, watching a character go through one tragedy after another. It's an outrageous story and hard to believe I could survive.

Shelley and I made the best of a horrible situation and spent some time in Spokane, Washington, before flying back home. When I look back on everything that had happened to me over the course of six weeks in the Northwest, I try to remember the positive things. Sometimes, even in the midst of my greatest challenges, I have chosen to see the glass as half full. I have found most situations aren't one hundred percent negative or one hundred percent positive. When all is said and done, it usually settles somewhere in between. How I remember my experiences depends on the focus of my lens. Sometimes surviving means finding the good in the worst of circumstances.

Much to my surprise, I was allowed to board an airplane with no driver's license and with an ankle monitor. Even though my attorney was confident I would not be convicted of any crimes, my case had to work its way through the criminal justice system. I was so embarrassed to pull up my pant leg and tell the TSA worker that I had paperwork from a judge for the monitor. He glanced down, and then looked at me and waved me through security. I doubt I was the first person he patted down with an ankle monitor.

We had a stopover in Denver on the way home, and they had several inches of snow pound the runway. While we waited in the airport, we had a call from my niece telling us that she had taken Mom to the emergency room. Sitting by the phone, waiting anxiously for me to call over several weeks, had unfortunately contributed to a blood clot in her leg.

Several hours after we left Denver and landed in Pittsburgh, we rushed to the hospital to see Mom. She was in good spirits, but they had admitted her so they could immediately start her on anti-coagulation medicine. I was almost in a state of shock, but in a functional kind of way.

The first night I slept in my king-size bed, I was overwhelmed by how good it felt. But when I closed my eyes, I saw flashes of the jail cell. The feeling of being trapped in a cage haunted me, and it would take quite some time before the memories faded. One of the things that really helped me was the therapy I'd had for PTSD. I learned how to stay in the present. Even when I had the worst of memories, I recognized they were memories, and this made it much easier to deal with.

A few days passed, and Mom was released from the hospital. The doctor said the blood clot was one of the worst he had ever seen. I could not help but feel guilty for causing her and the rest of my family members so much stress. Had anything happened to Mom, I would never have forgiven myself.

Chapter 20

Picking Up the Pieces

Within ten days, I found myself in the waiting room of yet another psychiatrist. But seeing Dr. Maura Andronic was not as if I was seeing a stranger. She had been Mom's doctor for several years, and when Mom was not doing so well, I would go with her to her appointments. I knew Dr. Andronic, and I had a lot of respect for her.

When I walked into her office for the first time as a patient, I felt terribly heavy and lethargic. She initially kept me on the same medication regimen that had been prescribed in the Idaho hospital. As I told her what had happened, she simply nodded—not unnerved or surprised—and listened without judgment.

As part of the condition for my release from jail, I had to follow through with outpatient care. Every three months, Dr. Andronic wrote a letter giving the court an update about my treatment, including whether I was compliant. I want to say it wouldn't have mattered even if I weren't court ordered into treatment, because in Idaho I realized how important it was for me to take medication for bipolar disorder. However, given my history, I feel overwhelmingly blessed to have been given the option of either treatment or jail. Many people don't get that choice. Whether I would have complied on my own is irrelevant because, the way I saw it, I never had the option, and rightfully so.

For most of the first year, I saw Dr. Andronic every month. Unlike many of my former psychiatrists, she spent as much time with me as I needed. Most of the time this meant well over the usual fifteen-minute allotment for medication checks. The first questions she always asked were, "How are you doing?" and "How much are you sleeping?" In the four years I've been seeing Dr. Andronic, I have never experienced another manic or psychotic episode. The medications she prescribes work well for me, and when they need adjusting, she is quick to suggest a new treatment plan.

After seeing Dr. Andronic for several years, I couldn't help but wonder what would have happened to my life had I seen her years ago. It had never entered my mind to see her as my psychiatrist. I didn't even think she would take me as a patient, because she was treating my mother, but she worked with me to improve my functionality and quality of life. I never had a doctor tell me I could recover; she was the first to do that. When I didn't have much hope, she told me it was the nature of the illness. She explained bipolar disorder, listened to my symptoms, and only once do I remember her getting frustrated with me and my persistence that I wanted to be symptom free.

My relationship with Dr. Andronic is so different from that with Dr. Martin, and I couldn't help but draw comparisons. Dr. Martin had specialized in child psychiatry and had been in private practice for general psychiatry when I started seeing her. I believe Dr. Martin wasn't experienced enough with bipolar disorder to treat me. I only wish I had known this before. I could have saved myself a mound of money and probably an even greater amount of heartache.

Along with Dr. Andronic, I also was seeing a therapist. Megan helped me work through the barrage of bad memories. I became more adept in dealing with and managing bipolar disorder. The more I could talk about symptoms, the easier it became to monitor them.

What I have learned the hard way is the more I stay on top of my illness, the better chance I have of living a healthy life. I never let more than one day go by without sleeping a significant amount. For me, lack of sleep was always the number one precursor to a manic and psychotic episode. On the other end, I know if I'm sleeping more than twelve hours, I'm probably struggling with the symptoms of depression. Dr. Andronic told me there are lots of medicines that effectively treat mania and psychosis, but far fewer that work for depression. Depression is the hardest part of the illness to treat.

With an excellent doctor and therapist on board, I was able to use my own research skills to better understand bipolar disorder. I read countless articles from a variety of authors about the illness. I devoured information and the *Life Unlimited Stories* from the Depression and Bipolar Support Alliance (DBSA) website. These stories gave me hope for recovery.

When I attended a DBSA annual meeting, I met a gentleman who became my friend. I told him my story of losing jobs, isolation, and trouble with the law. He said, "Welcome to the club." He told me when he went into the psychiatric hospital after a mental health crisis, he had a wife, a home, children, and a job, but when he came out of the hospital, he had nothing. It was incredibly sad to hear his story, yet the threads of how severe mental illness can have such tragic impact on lives really drove home the point that I needed to follow my treatment plan.

One of my biggest fans was my nephew, who constantly asked where I was during those three months away from home. He made a ring for me with a little note attached that said, "Love is number 1!" I still get a tear in my eye when I see it hanging in my office.

Perhaps what I had more than anything else was a loving family. I was not in contact with any friends, except for Julie, who had called while I was in the hospital. I stayed off social media for a very long time because I wanted to make sure I was completely stable before posting something on Facebook that I might regret—like when I had taken to Twitter in a manic racing thoughts rant one evening about politics. The funny thing is I ended up with a lot more Twitter followers. I closed my Twitter account and just recently created a new one.

Unfortunately, dealing with often embarrassing behavior can require cleaning up the mess after a major episode. That meant facing and being accountable for everything I did while

I was ill. I believe in accountability for my actions, even if I wasn't mentally well at the time. Equally, I hope others take into account that I did not understand what I was doing. If I did, we wouldn't be having this conversation.

My attorney worked with the prosecutor and had all the charges against me dropped. As much as I thought my situation in Phoenix could have had a better outcome, I knew how fortunate I was with my legal issues in Montana. I will be forever grateful to my attorney Kurt for his relentless support of me. Life could have been a whole lot different right now, and I don't mean in a positive way.

One of the first things I started doing was going to the gym for exercise. I went with my niece Natalie, and she helped me stay motivated and positive. Natalie would call to get me out of bed, and then come and pick me up to take me to the gym.

I was initially struggling with the sedation effects of the medication. I felt like a zombie, sleeping fourteen to fifteen hours a day and still feeling tired. It would take me over a year to find a medication with less sedating effects.

Crying did not come easily because some of the medications I was taking numbed my emotions. A flat effect, a reduction in emotional expression, does not lend itself to feeling deep, raw emotions. Some of the psychotropic medications have this effect. More than anything, I was angry with myself. I continued to tell myself I should have known better.

My anger was turned inward, but eventually I stopped being angry with myself, and I started being angry with God. I said to God, "I haven't been perfect, but I have been a good person. Why did you let this happen to me?" At one point, prayer had been what saved me, and then I began to unload all my feelings of guilt and self-pity on the doorstep of God.

Years later, when speaking to a friend about how angry I was with God, she said, "Don't worry, he can take it." That one comment softened my heart and eventually led me back to church and a renewed relationship with God. One of my favorite verses is Proverbs 4:23. "Above all else, guard your heart, for it is the wellspring of life." Everything I had been through took a toll on my heart, but the insight of my friend roused my faith and helped me heal.

A few months after I returned home, my niece planned a family vacation at the Outer Banks in North Carolina, and I decided to go. This period of time started what I would call "my awakening." There were so many bad things that had happened in my life, I had forgotten about all the good. It had been five years since I had taken a vacation. As a family, we went to the beach often when I was child, and as an adult, I had been to several different beaches. I always marveled at the sight of the water.

The ocean represents an amazing spiritual experience for me. I could sit for hours listening to the crashing waves, mesmerized by the rhythmic thumping of water rushing onto the shore. The very essence of peaceful tranquility filled up my mind with each passing day.

One afternoon, my niece Ashley and I were swimming in the ocean. We got caught in a riptide that was pulling us out into the deeper waters. The more I tried to swim against the current, the worse the pull seemed. Eventually, I remembered from lifeguard training years ago to swim diagonally.

After I had time to think about that tough swim, I was struck with an analogy. Fighting the current in the ocean was similar to how I felt when I was fighting the bipolar disorder diagnosis. If I continued to fight and deny, I was going to drown. When I learned to accept and go with the flow, I would be okay. Bipolar disorder is like the ocean to me. I have learned not to fear it, but to have a great respect for it.

We stayed at the beach for a week, and I left better off than when I arrived. It was a powerful place to begin the long journey of healing that was in front of me.

Chapter 21

Fighting for Normalcy

By the end of the summer, I was adamant about finding a job. I knew it was imperative for me to have interactions with other people to fully recover. I submitted my resume for various jobs online, but my employment history now had enormous gaps. Shelley had been working at a local retail store, what she called her "fun job," and said she could help me get hired there. I had never worked in retail, but I did own my Quzinos sandwich business, so I had an idea of what working in retail might be like.

One evening, she brought home an application for me. I filled out the application, and out of habit, I put the six-figure amount in the box for previous income. When Amy, the store manager, interviewed me, she said, "I hope you know we can't pay you the kind of money you used to make. Our pay is $7.25 an hour."

"No problem," I answered, without any hesitation.

I started working about ten hours a week. Everything I did took a little longer at first. My head was still a bit foggy from medications and all that I had been through. But the interaction with customers and other employees made all the difference in the world. By the time the holiday season rolled around, my cashier skills were ready for Black Friday.

The more hours I worked, the more my mental health improved, and I started to long for additional challenges. For many years I had written as a hobby, so after reading several mental health advocate blogs, I started one of my own called *Shedding Light on Mental Illness*. At first, I was very reluctant about putting my real identity online. My initial posts were also cautiously measured. I didn't share very much information about myself, and I wrote more from the third person.

At this time, I was also following the health of my former coach, Pat Summitt. She had made an announcement in 2011 that she was diagnosed with Alzheimer's disease. When she could no longer coach, she started the Pat Summitt Foundation with a mission to fund Alzheimer's research. Watching how Pat handled her illness provided me with a blueprint for how I could handle my own. She could have privately dealt with her illness, but instead, she reached out in ways that would help other people for years to come. I challenged myself and asked what I could do to reach back and help other people.

After about two months, I became more confident with my writing, and I started to share personal stories. The people who read, followed, and commented on my blog gave me the support and encouragement I needed to continue building my confidence. I really can't say enough positive things about blogging and reading the blogs of other mental health advocates.

The following winter Natalie asked me to chaperone a group of high school students she was taking to Europe. I was thrilled to cross the pond again. It had been over fifteen years since I had been in Paris, and I welcomed the opportunity to return. I had never been to Italy or spent much time in England, so I was very excited. Not to mention, interacting with young people has always lifted me up. It was a trip I will always be grateful for.

During the trip, every adult had a roommate, and I was fortunate to have Lynette as mine. She is Natalie's second cousin, and a highly energetic woman and great traveler who often joined local schools on trips abroad. The first night, we stayed up all night talking about a number of different things like schoolgirls. She was sitting on her bed and I on mine, having a deep and intense conversation, and I ended up spilling my guts and telling her about my bipolar disorder.

"I haven't shared this with very many people, but I have bipolar disorder," I said, nearly choking the words out of my mouth.

Lynette simply nodded.

I continued, "I take medications, but they make me feel like a zombie."

"Have you asked your doctor if you can take something different?" she asked.

"We're working on it. But it takes forever to change a medication."

"You seem like you're doing well. I would never have known if you didn't tell me."

That was music to my ears. I had become "normal" again, which to me meant people could not tell I had a mental illness.

I never went into any detail, but talked about how I was managing my illness. The next morning, I was so paranoid that I didn't get any sleep. Always in the back of mind was one thought. *Am I manic?* Lack of sleep has been my biggest trigger for episodes. Later, I went back to my room to take a nap and to deal with the time change and the excitement of disclosing my illness.

London is a fascinating city. It is rich with history and incredible architecture. The students learned a lot, but I believe we all walked away with a bit more culture and a lot more education.

I found myself caught between the present and the past at times. The effects from the all the tragic experiences were going to take a long time to heal. When other adults talked about their work or careers, I found myself drifting off to what had happened to me. I would go back in my mind to the years I could relate to professionals, but it felt like a lifetime ago. It was as if I had lived the lives of two different people, and the memories I had would have to be integrated in order for me to completely heal.

After a few days in London, we boarded a ship to cross the English Channel. The ship brought back wonderful memories of my days traveling with the team handball squad. In my first trip overseas with the team, we had taken a ship across the North Sea from Oslo, Norway, to Denmark. Being aboard that ship stimulated my thoughts from those days of becoming an Olympian. It was a surge of positivity I needed.

The last time I had been to Paris, I was with a group of friends, and we didn't have much time to spend sightseeing. Traveling with a group of students is all about viewing every possible sight. The best part was watching the kids' faces light up at the Louvre, one of the world's largest museums, while they took selfies with the Mona Lisa. I was taking in so much information and processing it. My mind was officially back in business.

By the time we got to Rome, I was exhausted. The medication side effects were beginning to take a toll, and the early morning schedule and hours of sightseeing were hard on me. I remember trying to stay awake on the bus from Pisa to Florence, but I was so tired I fell asleep sitting up.

* * *

Days before I left for Europe, I decided to make a trip to the animal shelter. I had been without a dog for quite a while.

Though I still had my cat, Mr. Kitty, I missed having a dog. I was only going to the shelter to look, but ended up coming home with a new dog named Brownie. He is a brown and black speckled beagle mix and nowhere near as obedient as any of my other dogs, but once I get attached, there is no going back, no matter how bad his behavior has been.

While I was in Europe, Mom took care of Brownie. By the time I arrived home, Brownie was on a short list for being returned to the shelter. Even though we have a fenced yard, Brownie managed to find his way under the fence and out into the woods. There is nothing or no one who can keep beagles from following their noses.

After a year or so of being quite wild, Brownie turned into a fantastic companion and another one of my kids. He helped me mend my broken heart. From day one, Brownie was a snuggler. Even at forty pounds, he always managed to find my lap. I did not have a lap dog since Wiggley, and of course my hundred-plus-pound lab Goldie. I cannot say enough good things about pets.

When I returned from Europe, I went back to work. I also started to research mental health advocacy organizations. I read everything I could find about different organizations and what their missions were. I decided on the National Alliance on Mental Illness (NAMI) because there's an affiliate in my hometown.

I went to one of their meetings and said, "I'm Amy. I have bipolar disorder. I want to be a mental health advocate." A few months passed, and NAMI of Greater Wheeling asked me to speak at their upcoming candlelight vigil service. I was very honored to speak and looked forward to re-energizing my speaking abilities.

What was challenging about telling my story was deciding what to reveal and what to hold close to my heart. It was extremely difficult because I tend to be an authentic person. For my speech, I decided I would tell the story of when I was first diagnosed with bipolar disorder. The talk was well received. People were sad I had lost my job because of a mental illness, but I couldn't imagine how they would have responded if I had told them more.

During this time, I also decided I needed another job. The one I had was great, but I didn't work enough hours. I wanted to challenge myself to work twenty hours a week. I believed if I kept pushing myself to get well, I would be able to experience a full recovery.

I was hired rather quickly at a large retail shoe store, working the closing shift. The first night at the end of the shift I was handed a vacuum cleaner. My job was to vacuum the entire store. I remember thinking to myself, "How can a person with a master's degree be in this position?" But then I focused on the purpose of working. After nearly a year of vacuuming, I actually learned to like it because it kept me busy.

One thing I had to overcome was worrying about what people thought if they saw me working in the shoe store. Not everyone knew I was an Olympian, but it's a small town, and quite a few people did know me. I never once thought I was too good for working in retail, but I did think about how it looked to other people. Even as I told myself I was being paranoid, in my self-conscious way, I wondered if people knew what my journey had been. As if they could look at me and recite all the ordeals I had been through.

As it turned out, it was really about my own insecurities and the way I judged success. Admittedly, there is big difference between working for some of America's largest companies and vacuuming the carpet at the shoe store. But I have learned that no matter how I have been taught to measure success, every job is important to our society. And at that time in my life, having a schedule and commitments was what I needed most.

I felt strongly about sharing with some of the people I worked with that I have bipolar disorder. The most amazing thing was they never treated me any differently. It was like people were saying everyone has something they are dealing with, and if they tell you they don't, it's probably a lie.

On my fiftieth birthday, Mom, Shelley, my niece Ashley, and I went to Las Vegas to celebrate. It was hard to believe my life had dramatically changed from two years prior. I had the opportunity to visit some of the places I had lived while working in Las Vegas, and every step along my journey became fuel to continue along the path of recovery.

Yet sometimes it seemed that for every step forward I went, I took two steps back. I wrote about my frustrations on my blog with titles like "Bipolar Disorder Cheated Me." I did feel cheated. I felt like I had done almost everything I was supposed to do, and things still did not work out the way they should have. Except I know better. I know that should've, would've, could've are meaningless words. Intellectually, I knew if I stayed stuck in self-pity it would inhibit me from getting well. I was determined to change my way of thinking to a healthier and more positive outlook.

* * *

Many spiritual teachers focus on staying in the present moment. For those who don't live with bipolar disorder, it's still a great challenge not to hold on to past mistakes and regrets. Because of my encounters with the criminal justice system, it was extraordinarily difficult for me to let go of the past. I beat myself up for a long time with negative judgments about how I could have handled bipolar disorder differently. I blamed myself relentlessly. I was plagued with guilt, and it was all baggage from the past.

While I knew it wasn't healthy to hold on to the past, and certainly even less healthy to ruminate about it, I found it difficult not to get stuck in a time when life was easier. Sometimes I have those moments when living in the present actually triggers my thoughts and takes me back to a different time and place.

I have wondered at times where I would be in life if I didn't have bipolar disorder. This mental war doesn't happen often, but it does affect me occasionally. I realized this when I started paying more attention to my thoughts. A little thought monitoring in an attempt to stay more in the present led me to realize how much I was dipping back into the past.

The balancing side to all of this is that I did benefit at times because of the extra energy I had from hypomania. But with the severe depression that usually followed a manic episode of any extreme, I don't really consider bipolar disorder a positive aspect of my life. In fact, I would trade all my athletic achievements and experiences for the chance to have had a life without the hardships caused by bipolar disorder. All the awards, adulation, individual and team achievements, the things most athletes dream about—I would give them all up in a heartbeat to have lived a "boring" life. Certainly, one without the extreme highs and lows of an undertreated and untreated mental illness.

I clearly understand we don't get to choose what ailment we get. But my severe bipolar disorder took such a great toll on every aspect of my personality—pride, ego, confidence, self-esteem—it seemed like I was constantly recovering from one episode to the next.

Truthfully, through extensive meditation and prayer, I came to a peaceful place when I realized I could use my experiences to help other people. Although I am by no means a celebrity, I have walked in some interesting circles. If I can continue to use my platform, persevere, teach others about mental illness, work to eliminate stigma, and share my story of recovery in hopes of making a positive impact in others' lives—it will make everything I have been through worth the long, difficult journey it has been.

There have been times when I felt I had to try to make sense of my bipolar episodes and the subsequent fallout. There were days when it made me so tired I'd often find myself going back to bed just to stop the unwanted memories.

I do consider myself a relatively positive person, but I have realized the traumas and the struggles with bipolar depression have caused me to be cynical at times, though most of the cynicism has evaporated as I have gotten well. I never sat around waiting for the other shoe to drop, but as I became more aware of my thoughts, it shed some light on the occasional disappointing views I was holding close inside. What I have noticed is the more I heal, the more hopeful and positive I become.

I have always been a dreamer, and there was a time when I could no longer find a dream. I would not let myself imagine possibilities. Then one Christmas I was spiritually moved, and I began to dream again. I was sitting in the living room in total darkness except for the blinking of the Christmas lights. Red, green, yellow, and blue were sparkling magically. I started praying. The place in my spirit where I had allowed my hopes and dreams to be kept was closed off by a cement vault with thick steel and a chain-locked fence. All I asked in my prayers was to allow me to dream again.

Tears started to gently stream down my cheeks. Emotions were frequently hard to come by, so when a tear leaked out, it was a time to celebrate. For them to pour down my face was a reason to jump up and down with joy. I often equate having an emotional moment with having a spiritual experience. I was clearly touched by the power of prayer.

I hold hope that my dreams will come true, even if those dreams consist of simple, everyday living that inspires my soul, and not elaborate dreams that go up in smoke after a manic episode. The truth is, through the proper treatment and a wellness plan, I am blessed without having mania, and that is surely a plus. Now I focus on reconciling my past and staying in the present without giving too much credence to wishing my life was different.

Paying attention to my thoughts has been a big part of my recovery. For the most part, I stay positive and hopeful even though I have my challenges. It's not an easy task to stay in the present moment, but it is where life takes place. As I have grown healthier mentally and spiritually, I have found it much easier to live in the present and with a sparkling eye focused on a dream of becoming a national speaker one day.

Years ago, I read countless books on self-help strategies. I read about living a balanced life and living in the present. I believed wholeheartedly in the concept of mind, body, and spirit. Except, my mind had let me down, my spirit was wounded, and my body took a beating. And in spite of it all, I never gave up.

Chapter 22

Mental Health Advocacy

After I returned from Las Vegas, I was invited to join the NAMI Greater Wheeling board of directors. I was thrilled. I wanted to work as a mental health advocate, and becoming more involved with NAMI was the avenue I needed to expand my efforts.

During my first board meeting, I hardly said one word. I felt self-conscious, and I lacked confidence. It was like I was stuck between two different worlds—one where I gave presentations and consulted on projects, and the other where I spent time in a jail cell because of my severe undertreated bipolar disorder. The vast differences in experiences prove invaluable to my mental health advocacy work.

At the board meeting, long-time member Jerry asked me to lead the Community Outreach Committee. He asked if I had ideas on what I might do. I suggested targeting college students with an educational presentation on mental illness—largely because I knew fifty percent of all mental illness begins by the age of fourteen, and seventy-five percent by the age of twenty-four. College age is the prime time for developing a problem, especially because there are no many triggering stressors.

"What kinds of things do you have in mind?" Jerry asked.

"I want to teach them one in five Americans live with mental illness. What the common signs and symptoms are, and the fact help is available, and treatment works. I want them to know there is no shame in having a mental illness."

"Why don't you put together a presentation and present it at the next NAMI meeting?"

"You mean...like a PowerPoint presentation?"

"I don't know. What did you have in mind?"

"A PowerPoint. Definitely a slide presentation." And my mind began to trail off and think about how rusty my skills were. But I reassured myself I could do it, and all the board members were extremely supportive.

The next day I sat down at the computer and began researching. It reminded me of my days of working in corporate America. If there was a hot topic at work and I didn't know much about it, I would research until I became knowledgeable and could participate in in-depth discussions. The skills I learned were a bit rusty, and it took a little longer to complete tasks, but I was determined to do it.

I was given a list of people in the community who might be interested in my talk, and I invited several of them. Twenty-six people showed up, which was more than I anticipated.

As I stood in front of the room, I was quite nervous. My mother, Shelley, Aunt Priscella, Uncle Sam, and my cousin Keely were all there to support me. I fidgeted with my slide advancer in my hands, and leaned back forth from one leg to the other.

I knew the material well and had practiced for hours. I stood in my home office going through each slide and determining what I was going to say. I might not have been presenting to an Executive Board, but it was still very important to me.

Once I got going, I had no problem. The main negative feedback I received was that I didn't share anything about my own journey. People love stories. Stories resonate in ways that all the best information in the world cannot. I took the feedback and started to incorporate telling various aspects of my story to different audiences. It has been very powerful.

One of the NAMI board members had a son who worked for the local newspaper. The board thought having a sports writer do a story about my talks might help more people in the community become interested. When I first saw the headline in the paper, I was shocked. "Ex-John Marshall Star Amy Gamble's Toughest Foe Was Mental Illness." It's one thing to write a blog about mental illness in the world of social media, but it's another to have your mental illness publicly stated in a small-town newspaper. Though I felt very strongly about what I was doing and how I now had the ability to help people because of my platform, it took me a couple of days to get past my insecurities.

There have been other people who were willing to share their struggles and triumphs of living with a mental illness. I had examples to follow. If I was going to become a bigger advocate or activist and help eliminate stigma, I needed to become okay with people knowing I had bipolar disorder. This was a turning point for me in my recovery. I was accepting myself for all of who I had become. Including the hardships I had lived through.

I was asked to give my next talk at the local middle school to an audience of three hundred students. I decided to tell them that I lived with a mental illness, and I told some of my stories from my college days. I didn't expect the students to have any questions at the end, but when more than twenty-five hands went up, I was taken aback. I learned that young people want to talk about mental illness.

After I answered questions, the students were dismissed. I was shocked when about fifteen students stayed behind to talk with me. Some wanted to talk about the Olympics, but one girl wanted to tell me she struggled with suicidal thoughts.

She said, "Every day I walk home from school across the bridge, I want to jump off and die. I can't get these thoughts out of my head."

I was struck by how real her pain was to her, and I understood because I had been there myself. But I was caught off guard when a twelve-year-old girl I didn't know told me she wanted to die by suicide.

I stood there calmly and said, "I want you to know that your life matters. You are important. I know it's hard now, but you're going to overcome your feelings. Let's talk with one of your teachers and see if we can get you some help."

"No. I don't want anyone to know," she said, nearly in tears.

I replied, "Telling people is the first step in making those thoughts go away."

"Okay," she reluctantly agreed, and I went and found the school nurse. I explained the situation, and she took it from there.

* * *

In March 2015, my friend Betsy's church was having a special event. They were bringing in a national speaker from Florida. I had never been to The Experience Church before, but I had heard about it. I knew it was different from the Lutheran church I had grown up in. It was one night, I told myself, one night. What could that hurt?

Much to my surprise, the woman who was speaking lived with bipolar disorder. She discussed her challenges and what her life looked like in the present. It was one thing to read people's stories, and another to listen to a speaker. I knew I was not alone in the battle against bipolar disorder. Other people had their battle stories to tell and scars to show.

After her talk, I stood in line to meet her. I told her I lived with bipolar disorder and wanted to become a speaker. She encouraged me. Later I would send her an email and tell her a little bit about myself. She suggested I find a Bible-based church to help with my healing.

I started attending The Experience Church. My heart was still broken, and I felt closed off spiritually. I believed in God, but my anger and emotions had to go somewhere, and I turned all the negative emotions toward God. I continued to ask the question, "Why me?"

Pastors Tim and Linda Seidler of The Experience Church asked me to do a testimony during the church services. The church is one that utilizes creativity to get the message of Christ across to a broad range of followers. They do not hesitate in talking about any subject, and mental illness was a topic they wanted to tackle.

My testimony at church was not only about the hardships, but also about hope. I shared that I had lost everything when I lost my job as a result of bipolar disorder, and that was a difficult statement for me to make. There were about eight hundred people who heard me that day. I wasn't sure if I made a difference in other people's lives, but it had made a difference in mine. In my mind, I released this secret I had been holding on to for a very long time.

Holding secrets is like picking up a basket of apples and realizing they are all rotten. It is the disappointing feeling you get when you realize you can't take a bite out of the apple, and now you have to deal with the gross remnants. Untold stories rot inside and steal energy. Releasing the secrets is like throwing all the apples away at one time and having space for a new basket.

I began attending church on a regular basis. Prayer correlated with healing. The more I prayed, the more I healed. I found the people at church to be kind and supportive. Every week I took myself to church, I healed a little more, and my heart began to open once again.

As part of my work as an advocate, I wanted to provide educational programs for the community. One gentleman who attended my presentation encouraged me to become an instructor for Mental Health First Aid. He had a contact in Houston, Texas, who he told me to call.

I spoke to a woman named Suzette. She is a high-energy champion of Mental Health First Aid and a national trainer for this very important class. Mental Health First Aid is an eight-hour certification course that teaches people how to help someone who is either developing a mental illness or who is in a crisis. It was developed in Australia and is now taught in twenty-three countries around the world. I firmly believe education is one of the ways to change minds. We cannot eliminate stigma unless people are better informed about mental illness and know what to do to help someone through a difficult time.

Traveling to Houston was the first trip I had taken by myself in seven years. In my professional career, I had traveled extensively, so when I stepped into the airport alone, it was like putting on an old pair of shoes. Familiar. Confidence-building. Another step forward in my recovery journey. I felt like my life had a purpose.

Sponsored in part by the National Council on Behavioral Health, the Mental Health First Aid instructor training was among the best training I have ever had. Considering I had worked for the number one Fortune 500 company, I had been a part of excellent training in the past, and I had something to compare the program to.

On the last two days of the course, each of us had to present part of the training to our peers. I had this underlying confidence, but I felt like I was a newborn foal with wobbly legs. I practiced for hours the evening before I gave my presentation. We were all graded using a Rubric methodology. In other words, how well did we present? Did we meet the objectives?

I was given glowing feedback on my presentation and facilitation skills. What the trainer didn't know was I had been a professional facilitator when I did consulting work a few years back. Like every other skill I had, everything was just a bit rusty. The folks in Houston could not have been nicer. I told many of them I lived with bipolar disorder. They never blinked an eye.

I had dinner with my friend Jacinda, who had recently finished a doctorate in clinical psychology. We were talking about my work at the shoe store, and she pointed out that I was underemployed. I never told her how I ended up in that position. I didn't say how guilty I felt for not better managing bipolar disorder.

In moments when I feel deeply connected to another person, I wanted to be authentic. It's a lonely road carrying such a heavy secret. My dilemma was fearing I would be judged harshly. How could I not judge myself? It seemed I had every opportunity to get a handle on my bipolar disorder.

Then, in a moment of reflection, I realized it was not under my control. I was not the only person who needed to be held responsible for what happened to me. I knew I was walking a fine line between being a victim of circumstances and being accountable for my own actions. I would have to find a healthy balance if I wanted peace of mind.

* * *

The first Mental Health First Aid class I taught was to a group of college seniors in an abnormal psychology class. I was nervous when I first stood in front of the room and had eighteen young people eagerly awaiting what I had to say. The students were not as interactive as I would have liked. However, feedback I received from one of the students said, "College students don't volunteer. You have to call on us to make us talk. Maybe this will help in your next class."

One of the best parts of teaching the course is getting feedback at the end of the class. I always utilize the comments and suggestions to improve my skills as an instructor. And it doesn't hurt to have positive feedback either. In fact, the positive feedback fed directly into my confidence building efforts.

Each class I taught left me feeling like I had made a small difference in the fight against mental illness stigma. Not only was I teaching, I was learning about myself. The more classes I taught, the stronger I became. I was driven to become a mental health advocate so I could help other people. At the end of the day, I was also helping myself.

A year later, I had taught twelve Mental Health First Aid classes. In between the classes, I made another trip to Houston to get certification in the youth curriculum. In a short time, I had taken a horrifically challenging situation and learned how to make the best of it. All my mistakes in how I handled bipolar disorder became my fuel for educating others. If I could save only one person from a fraction of the heartache I experienced, it would all be worth it.

I will continue to passionately work to bring awareness for mental illness so people will not feel ashamed to get help. The stigma of mental illness is a dark shadow causing tragic outcomes for far too many people. My mission in life is to contribute in some small way to eliminating the darkness and bringing mental illness into the light.

Chapter 23

My Friend Hunter

One fall morning as I was getting ready for work, I received a call from my cousin Bonnie. She knew I had struggled with bipolar disorder and that I'd become a mental health advocate.

Bonnie said, "I have a friend from high school who has a son in jail because of bipolar disorder. I was calling to ask you if you would write to him in jail."

I didn't hesitate and wasn't surprised. Having had my own encounters with the criminal justice system, I knew firsthand severe bipolar disorder could wreak some havoc.

"Sure, I'll write to him."

Later in the day, I received a private Facebook message from Hunter's mom, who gave me his address. She thanked me for being willing to write to him.

Hunter was in jail as a result of what happened during a psychotic episode. He had been taking a low dose of medication, but not the usual combination of medications that those of us with severe bipolar disorder need. He didn't hurt anyone, but he did run into their cars in a drive-through, and in the state of California, that is assault with a deadly weapon.

We started writing letters, and I found Hunter to be a brilliant young man who had unfortunately been afflicted with bipolar disorder. He had maintained a 4.0 GPA at the University of Colorado and had successfully completed three years. Then his mental health started to interfere with his life to the point he dropped out of college.

Hunter has a wonderful family, lots of support, and had an excellent attorney. He was found not guilty by reason of insanity on all charges. After a very long and trying eighteen months in jail, he was released to the custody of the state mental institution where he is currently receiving treatment. It is unclear how long he will have to stay in the state hospital.

It's hard to believe a bright, twenty-seven-year-old man with a tremendous amount of opportunities could end up in the situation Hunter did. However, this can be the nature of untreated or undertreated bipolar disorder. Not everyone will end up entangled in the legal system, but many people do. In fact, more lives than we will ever know are entrenched in the legal system due to severe mental illness.

I believe some advocates could do a better job of talking about the realities of severe mental illness. People need to understand the potential consequences for those who don't get the proper treatment. I get very frustrated with the people who advocate against taking medication because I know firsthand what happened to me without these potentially life-saving drugs.

Some would argue having an open dialogue about these issues only feeds into the stigma of mental illness. I believe ignoring the problem will not make it go away. Using stories as examples of what can happen is a good step in the right direction to help people to understand—particularly when it comes to psychosis. Psychosis is the most misunderstood aspect of mental illness, and as a culture we absolutely must have open conversations about it.

Hunter and I now speak on the phone a few times a month. If you had a conversation with him, you would never know he has a mental illness. It's my hope he will someday leave the state institution and develop his life. I always tell him he would make a good advocate because he understands the consequences and could help other people avoid the agonizing pain he has been through. I also hope he is given the chance to take his life back. It would be another tragedy to see him living his life in an institution.

In fact, one of the reasons I decided to open up about my legal issues is because of a conversation I had with Hunter.

"So…what are you up to lately? My life is pretty much the same every day. Tell me about yours," Hunter said during a phone conversation.

"Well, I've developed a presentation for college students…"

He interrupted, "Did you tell them about being in jail?"

"I haven't given the talk yet."

"You gotta tell them about the jail thing. They really won't understand if you don't. I think it's better to be authentic. Think of the people you can help. Think of the people like me."

"I'll have to think about it. It doesn't make me very comfortable talking about it."

"Yeah. Well, you were sick when it happened. How can people understand if you don't talk about it?"

"I'll think about it."

"Let me know how it goes."

I thought about it overnight, and the next few days I began writing a talk utilizing my story from jail. How I got there. Why it was so important to get help as soon as a person had early symptoms. The conversation also affected my writing. It allowed me to tell the *whole* story and not simply the comfortable parts. Writing the story became part of the healing process.

Hunter's story puts a name on a statistic. His life matters. He has a mother and father who care deeply about him. How long will he have to stay in the state institution? Being found not guilty by reason of insanity has made him a ward of the state, which means his treatment time could end up even longer than a prison sentence. I am certain if I knew more of Hunter's story, he likely had several opportunities along the way to get the help he needed, including being educated about his illness. People need to know serious mental illness must be treated, and most often treatment includes the right combination of medications.

Chapter 24

The Sun Shines Again

Sometime in January 2016, my old friend Charlotte got in contact with me through Facebook. Charlotte was one of my mentors when I worked in the pharmaceutical industry, and she always looked after me. She was and continues to be a strong female role model and a good friend. Charlotte was doing a special assignment in Philadelphia and asked me if I wanted to get together for a long weekend while she was there. My initial response was, "Sure." Then I wondered how it would be interacting with someone from my past who knew me before I had walked in hell. I was curious to know how she might perceive me. But I got past my worries, and we set a date to get together.

We met up over Easter weekend, which happened to be March Madness. We had endless conversations and fabulous meals and, surprisingly, I felt rather normal. The best part of the trip was going to the Philadelphia Performing Arts Center to see *Beautiful: The Carole King Musical.* It was as if the weekend awakened the sleeping positive memories of my past. All the tragedy I had experienced took up so much space in my mind that I failed to remember how much time I had spent enjoying life. Going to the theater had always been one of my favorite indulgences.

Charlotte was organizing a work reunion in Phoenix, and she wanted me to come. On the surface, I seemed confident and self-assured, but on the inside, I was holding this gigantic secret about my past. It wasn't until I was writing this book that I realized how much power it had over me. I felt like anyone who looked at me would know I had been through a lot. Truth be told, I didn't think I was good enough anymore to be in the company of professionals who held some very high positions in corporate America. What made the difference for me was when Mom told me I deserved to be there as much as anyone else, and she was proud of how far I had come. That struck a chord with me, like another part of me was waking up from a long, bad dream—except mine was a living nightmare.

* * *

When my plane landed in Phoenix, I had butterflies in my stomach. There were two things I noticed. One, the temperature was well over one hundred degrees, and even though people say it's a dry heat, it is hot. Two, after living back east in the green, lush landscape of trees, the brown desert looked shockingly sparse, as if it needed a drink of water.

I had not been in Phoenix since 2007 when I had to go before a judge. This time I was going to see old friends and colleagues from work. Four years prior, I would not have expected to have a full social calendar, but every single day, I had the opportunity to see old friends. I wanted to make another trip to the Grand Canyon, but my schedule was simply too full.

The best part of my visit was reconnecting with people. Bipolar disorder took its toll on my ability to maintain relationships. It was so special to discover my friends never stopped caring about me, and this was by far the greatest gift of all.

My primary reason for going to Phoenix was for the work reunion. It felt strange to go because I felt so far removed from my days in corporate America. I was hesitant to attend the party, not because I was ashamed of having a mental illness, but because I had gained so much weight from the medications.

In my professional days, I was known as the Olympian, and I had always stayed fit. But in spite of my insecurities, I showed up and interacted regardless of my waist size. To be honest, I really wanted people to see me healthy and to know a person with bipolar disorder can recover. They had no idea what I had been through and what courage it took to be in their presence. After the fact, it was confidence building, but leading up to it, I was very nervous. I knew my secrets, and they were weighing on my conscience.

The day before the reunion, I had an opportunity to visit a former colleague. We sat by the pool at a beautiful resort in Phoenix reminiscing about old times. Deb had been a triathlete, and at fifty-seven was still incredibly fit. She also knew the reality of weight gain from psychotropic drugs. I finally gathered my courage, and that afternoon Deb became the first person I told about what had happened to me in Montana. Never once did she make me feel "less than" or "crazy." At a very deep level, she understood it was an illness, and I happened to be one of the unlucky who inherited it.

What was most fascinating were the people who came up to me at the party to talk about how mental illness had impacted their lives or the lives of their loved ones. By the end of the evening I was glad I had come. Many folks encouraged me to keep up my work as a Mental Health Advocate. I appreciated their kind words.

Five days in Arizona went rather quickly, and when it was time to go, I felt a sense of peace come over me. It was a very spiritual and internal feeling of a balanced perspective, and I felt incredibly grounded. I boarded the plane headed for Las Vegas for the second part of my ten-day trip. Shelley was turning sixty, and she wanted to celebrate her birthday in one of her favorite places.

The first few days in Las Vegas began with an early morning cup of Starbucks and meeting Shelley and the gang at the Mandalay Bay swimming pool. Above anything else Vegas style, Mandalay Bay has cornered the market on pools. There are at least five pools, a lazy river, and a wave pool. We always staked out a place under a group of palm trees to give us a little shade from the afternoon sun.

We went out to dinner for her sixtieth birthday, and then everyone went to a lounge to have some drinks. While they all had beer and wine, I ordered a diet Coke. Ever since I had

returned from Montana, I rarely drank any alcoholic
beverages. It was part of a lifestyle change I made because I
learned it was not a good idea to mix psychotropic
medications and alcohol. The alcohol makes the medications
less effective, and alcohol is a depressant. I can get depressed
well on my own without it.

* * *

I stood in front of a crowd of more than two thousand
people and delivered an inspiring graduation speech. I poured
my heart out, telling the graduates everyone needs to have a
dream, and I am proof that dreams really do come true. But
sometimes we have to pick ourselves back up when we fall,
and other people might not support us, but persistence will
always lead to success. The headline in the paper read
"Olympian Tells Graduates to Follow Dreams." It has always
worked well for me.

When I said those words, the underlying meaning was so
powerful. At that time, only a few people knew about my
struggles with the legal system. I had shared many things with
audiences, but I had not shared what I considered my biggest
struggle.

With everything I had experienced, the message was not
only for the students, but for me as well. This is what
happens sometimes when we give—we receive a whole lot
more in return.

There was so much I wanted to tell the graduates. Had the
graduation happened five months later, I would have had
more to say. Why? Because I have been on this path toward
recovery, and every day I take one step forward to regaining
more confidence and self-esteem. Every day I move further
and further away from the distraught bipolar patient and
more toward the strong bipolar thriver I know I can be.

When I was asked to give the commencement speech, I
was extremely honored. Of course, no one really had any idea
of all the scrapes and bruises I had accumulated over the past

several years. My highlight reel appears pretty good from the outside looking in. However, my reality is far more about overcoming an extraordinary amount of adversity. My hope is that those who heard that graduation speech will know it was much deeper than it may have sounded.

My journey had been about extreme highs and lows, with bipolar disorder running the show. Now it's about living a peaceful existence and making a difference one person at a time, especially the person looking back at me in the mirror.

It has truly been a gift to be capable of recovering. Not many people who get to stage four of any illness are able to recover. But for some reason, in all my past experiences, the people I have met along the way, the endearing love and support from my immediate family, the blessings I have been given as part of my NAMI family, my church family, and those who have encouraged me, have all mattered and made a significant difference in my recovery.

Every encounter I have had with someone who has been kind to me, whether it was on social media or on a more personal level, has impacted my ability to recover. It has given me the strength to continue my journey with a renewed passion and a purpose. I only wish everyone who struggles with mental illness could be as fortunate as I have been as I fought my way back to a life worth living.

* * *

A young woman from New Hampshire, Sammy, came up to me after I gave a talk at a local college. She said, "I want you to know what a difference you just made in my life. I grew up watching my mom struggle with depression for years. After tonight, I have a better understanding of what she goes through. You may not know it, but what you say has an impact on people. I'm going to be a better and more supportive daughter because of what I learned tonight. Thank you."

I was grateful for the feedback because sometimes beating a mental health awareness drum can be very lonely, and I have wondered if I was really making a difference. Usually what happens to me is exactly the time I need to hear something positive, I will get a sign or a comment reinforcing that I am on the right track. I call this divine intervention.

My motto has been if I can make a difference in just one person's life, then everything I do to prepare and work at being a better mental health speaker is worth it. In fact, everything I have been through has served a purpose. It has given me the ability to relate and connect to other people in ways I would never have known possible. My greatest joys in life have never come from the accumulation of material things. What has mattered most has been the connection to other people. No amount of money can buy the power of inspiring and being inspired. In the magic of the moment, Sammy's words brought me a tremendous amount of healing and the reinforcement of what I have always known to be true—I can't change the past, but I can use the lessons to help myself and others.

It has been about two years since I first began working for NAMI of Greater Wheeling. In that time, I have spoken to over twenty-five hundred middle school, high school, and college students. My intention has been to educate young people to help eliminate stigma and make sure they know it is okay to get help. I will continue on this mission to make a difference for the rest of my life.

Chapter 25

The Recovery Journey

I was talking with a friend about writing this book and said, "It took so much determination to be able to recover, and honestly, I can tell you there were times when I wondered if I could. There were times when I really thought about giving up."

She looked at me with respect and said, "So, how did you do it? How did you recover?"

"Recovery is a lifelong journey. But I'm on the road," I replied.

Recovery is not a destination. It is constantly evolving your circumstances to get closer to living a "normal" life. To me, recovery is saying, "I deserve better," then focusing on doing all the things necessary to create a fulfilling life.

How did I pull myself up to reclaim and rebuild my life?

For me, one of the most powerful self-help strategies has been journal writing. I began writing in a diary in the seventh grade when my Aunt Mary Francis gave me a little blue diary with a lock and key I still have to this day. I continued writing throughout my life. My journals kept me sane when I was in jail. It kept me going when I struggled at Tennessee. It gave me freedom to express myself and my raw emotions. Now I use it to help manage my illness and tap into my creative space.

When people think of recovery, most of the time they think about addiction recovery. It is true there are many parallels between each kind of recovery. In fact, the Substance Abuse and Mental Health Services Administration (SAMHSA) combined their information on recovery to include both recovery from mental illness and substance use disorders. I found their Ten Guiding Principles of Recovery very helpful and informative.

SAMHSA's 10 Guiding Principles of Recovery:

- **Hope**—The belief that recovery is real provides the essential and motivating message of a better future—that people can and do overcome the internal and external challenges, barriers, and obstacles that confront them.
- **Many Pathways**—Individuals are unique with distinct needs, strengths, preferences, goals, culture and backgrounds—that affect and determine their pathways to recovery.
- **Peer Support**—Mutual support and mutual aid groups; including the sharing of experiential knowledge and skills, as well as social learning, play an invaluable role.
- **Culture**—Culture and cultural background in all of its diverse representations-including values, traditions, and beliefs—are keys in determining a person's journey.
- **Addresses Trauma**—The experience of trauma (such as physical or sexual abuse, domestic violence, war, disaster, and others) is often a precursor to or associated with alcohol and drug use, mental health problems, and related issues. Services and support must address trauma.
- **Respect**—Eliminating stigma and discrimination and protecting the rights of people who live with mental illness is important.
- **Strengths/Responsibility**—Individuals, families, and communities have strengths and resources that serve as a foundation for recovery.
- **Holistic**—Recovery encompasses an individual's whole life, including mind, body, spirit, and community.

- **Relational**—An important factor in the recovery process is the presence and involvement of people who believe in the person's ability to recover; who offer hope, support, and encouragement.
- **Person Driven**—Self-determination and self-direction are the foundations for recovery as individuals define their own life goals and design their unique paths towards those goals.

Above anything else, I had to have hope. I fully expected to recover. I didn't know exactly how it was all going to turn out, but I believed I was on a positive pathway. I hoped for good things to happen.

First of all, I recovered multiple times after many bipolar episodes including manic, depressive, and psychotic. It's an ongoing process when a person has a chronic mental illness. I imagine in my lifetime I will continue fighting the battle and working toward managing symptoms, and at times motivating myself to get out of bed, even when all I want to do is sleep off the depression. Recovery does not mean I am healed forever; it means I am living in remission. I have been enjoying nearly five years of stability. But even if I manage my illness carefully, I could have another episode. Most likely not a psychotic episode, because the medication controls it well, but certainly hypomania and depression are on the table. This is the harsh reality of bipolar disorder.

I believe medications are an imperative aspect of stable, prolonged recovery. Most people with bipolar disorder require medications to remain stable. I know many people don't like to take any kind of medicines, but if it comes down to having a relatively normal life or living in and out of institutions or jail, I believe the evidence speaks for itself. I was one of those people who learned this lesson the hard way.

As I told Hunter, "There have been times when I sat on the edge of my bed and debated whether to take the medication. I feel good. I think I can manage without it. And then suddenly my higher self kicks in and says, 'How did that work out for you in the past?' I take the pills."

I continued, "I take four medications for bipolar disorder. It can take some time to find the right combination that works. I worked with Dr. Andronic to find the right medications that would help me walk the fine line between having no manic episodes and being a zombie. Fortunately, we found the right combination."

He replied, "I get it."

I typically don't share what medication I take because what works for one person might not work for another. It's trial and error, and it sometimes takes a long time to get it all sorted out.

Beyond taking medication, I am a huge believer in therapy. With the right therapist, healing and recovery can happen much quicker, especially when learning positive coping strategies. I currently don't see a therapist on a regular basis, but when I need to, I don't hesitate to call.

My therapist helped me work through everything that happened to me. She did it with compassion, genuine care, empathy, and a little humor. One therapy session stands out in my mind.

I was telling Megan how I felt *small*, not confident and like people knew everything I had gone through. She had a table with four little chairs she used for the kids she saw in therapy. Megan looked at me while pointing at the kids' table and said, "It sounds like you think you're a little kid sitting at the table with pizza all over your face. I'm here to tell you that's not what anyone else thinks. I see you as strong and gifted, with lots of memorable experiences."

I started laughing with the clear visualization. This day was a turning point in my recovery. I will always be grateful to her.

Once I was working toward stable mental health, I began looking for the things most people take for granted. I wanted to work again. Even though I was by far underemployed, working at the shoe store provided interaction with other people and a way to build self-esteem and confidence.

One of the hallmark signs of mental illness is isolation. It makes the condition worse, and to get better, I had to get myself out of the house and interact with other people. I knew work would provide the opportunity to talk to people, even if that meant simply telling people to "Have a nice day!"

I sat down at my computer and wrote a plan focused on mind, body, and spirit. In SAMHSA's words, I took a "holistic" approach to recovery. The spiritual aspect of my recovery was a little tricky because without my faith, I would not be writing these words, and yet I was really angry with God. I felt like he gave me the short end of the stick.

To heal my spiritual self, I started out with a Bible study class with Pastor Paul Schafer. I learned a great deal, but I still felt my emotions and spirit were damaged. Even after the Bible study class, it took me over two years to start attending church. I enjoyed the messages that Pastor Tim and Linda Seidler gave so passionately. Months went by, and I kept listening and praying and hoping I would get a spiritual breakthrough.

Then one Sunday, Pastor Linda spoke about how there is "power in our past," and how we can reach back and help other people with what we have learned. I wanted to stand up in church and yell, "Yes! This message is for me!"

I'm a person who taps into all my resources, and for what I was going through, I felt like I needed additional pastoral counseling. I reached out to Pastor Sherri Schafer, Paul's wife. She recommended an excellent book called *Pastrix: The Cranky, Beautiful Faith of a Sinner and Saint* by Nadia Bolz-Weber. I would return to speak with Pastor Sherri on occasion and always left feeling my heart and soul were in a better place.

Some people don't do traditional church or even believe in a higher power. I could never have made it if I did not believe God had my back. I had too much pain, suffering, and issues to resolve and come to terms with. My spiritual self gave me the strength and confidence I needed to take the next steps in my journey.

I had learned some meditation techniques and had an audio version I listened to. This helped me clear my mind and thoughts. With the encouragement of Shelley, I also volunteered at a soup kitchen, and I would highly encourage people recovering to find a cause you care about. The benefits are a two-way street. Being engaged with other people helped me take the focus off my own challenges and cast my net in a bigger way. There was such an intrinsic value in helping other people.

I worked very hard at forgiving myself and others, letting the past go, and using the power of mindfulness and staying in the present moment. I used a gratitude journal in which I wrote down what I was thankful for. Sometimes, before I went to sleep, I thanked God for all the people and things I was grateful for.

One of the things I have learned is it is impossible to recover from mental illness without the help of other people. The times in my life when I had close relationships and friendships, my mental health was always much better. When I became isolated and had no one to look out for me, I struggled greatly. This is why peer support groups are so beneficial. Finding people who have recovered and who are strong enough to reach back and help others is invaluable.

At one point, I had watched a YouTube video created by the International Bipolar Foundation about the grieving process. It struck me I was not only dealing with depression, I was also grieving for the life I had lost, for the dreams shattered.

I looked up Elisabeth Kubler-Ross's five stages of grief. Grief was not an obvious emotion, but I later learned many people experience grief from receiving disappointing news about their health. Why would a mental illness diagnosis be any different?

The first stage of grief is denial. "Not me! This isn't happening to me!" Check. Been there, done that.

Second stage—anger. "Why me? Why is this happening to me?" Check.

Third stage is bargaining. "But what if I...I promise I'll be a better person if only..." Yep.

Fourth stage—depression. "Whatever, I don't care anymore."

Fifth stage—acceptance. The stage which says, "Okay, me; what's next? I'm ready for whatever comes."

I was beginning to teeter with the acceptance stage and eventually found my way to it. But the stages of grief are not linear. Even though I have accepted my situation and circumstances, every now and then I find myself at the second stage, "Why me?" It doesn't happen very often, but it creeps up from time to time.

What helped was finding other kindred spirits who were in varying stages of grief themselves. I went online and did Twitter chats with the people from This is My Brave, a non-profit organization working to eliminate stigma through storytelling performances. Once a month they host a Twitter chat where the participants answer various questions about things related to the struggle of mental illness and provide hope for each other. It was helpful hearing others' perspectives on what they were dealing with, and how I could apply what I was learning to my own journey.

I read countless books of other people who had recovered. *An Unquiet Mind: A Memoir of Moods and Madness* by Kay Redfield Jamison; *The Center Cannot Hold: My Journey Through Madness* by Elyn R. Saks, and more. I have a library full of books by people who have lived with mental illness and who have recovered and moved on to live very happy and successful lives.

I used visualization techniques I learned in college at the University of Tennessee to help improve my performance. I have sat and imagined myself happy, with lots of friends and engaged in the community. Whatever dream I have, I see myself achieving it. I want to become a National Mental Health Speaker, and I see the stage and the audience. I hear the applause. It's not a delusion; it is visualization. There is a difference.

When I need to feel inspired in the battle of recovery, I find an inspirational story about someone who has overcome something extraordinary. I put my challenges in perspective. I look to people like Nick Vujicic, a person who was born without any legs or arms and has become an international inspirational speaker and lives his life with grace and beauty. I can follow his lead.

Periodically, I used the video camera and made clips about where I was in the process of recovery. I also sat in front of the camera practicing for the day I would have the chance to stand in front of an audience and tell my story. I wanted to be able to look back and have proof of how far I had journeyed on the road to recovery.

When I gave a keynote speech about recovery, I included pictures of before, during, and after one of the greatest struggles of my life. The saying goes, "A picture is worth a thousand words." There is great truth in that. I like to show a picture of the present because it really demonstrates how far I have come and that there is hope for recovery.

I began to remember every experience that was positive in my life. It was as if the cobwebs were being removed from an attic stored with a lifetime of treasures. I realized in every corner of my soul, life is not in boxes of good and bad, black and white, but rather it is a continuum of various shades.

I read books on how to restore your confidence. Articles about having low self-esteem forced me to look at myself and make corrections. I learned about the grieving process, because I knew I was grieving for the life I had lost and for the dreams that were destroyed. I had to find a new sense of purpose to rejuvenate my soul.

Finding my sense of purpose was critical. For me, it came down to teaching and speaking because I could use my skills and experiences to help other people. As Ronald Reagan once said, "We can't help everyone, but everyone can help someone."

When I teach a course or give a talk, I always focus on the *one* person who may have needed to hear the message. My motto has been, "If I can help one person, everything I do is worthwhile."

Teaching Mental Health First Aid courses was a boost in a way I never imagined. Every class I taught grew my confidence tenfold. The best part was the evaluation form at the end of every class. I was told by more than three hundred people who took my classes that I was a pretty awesome instructor. That was more than a shot in the arm. I started to embrace the fact that I had something to offer others and it might be special. It helped to have people along my path encourage me.

Sometimes it would take many days and I would just grind away wondering if I could ever get a break. And then it would happen. I would have the *aha* moment and I would feel ten feet tall. I learned I could not feel the progress when I was in the midst of a struggle or a personal growth process. When the breakthrough came, all the pieces magically fit together like a puzzle. As I reflected, it sure seemed a lot easier than it was at the time I was trudging through.

There were times I had setbacks and I'd have to pull off the road and take a break. But I learned to tell myself I was going to feel better tomorrow. And I almost always did.

At the end of the day, my good friend Libby, a member of the NAMI Greater Wheeling Board of Directors, would remind me, "It doesn't matter where you have been or what circumstances caused you pain, it only matters where you are today. And I love you no matter what you have been through, and I will be there for you if you go through a tough time." Libby saying this to me was a gift I will always treasure. She and her husband George have been an amazing gift in my life.

From May 2015 to May 2017, I gave over seventy talks. I set out to help others, and the gift I was given in return was an empowering sense of pride, knowing I had done something good. I had educated over three thousand people on mental illness. My mission to help eliminate the ill effects of stigma was in progress. The more I talked, the healthier I became. All the negative energy bottled up inside was used to fulfill my passion. I now had a purpose far greater than myself. I could gently smile, knowing I had found my way.

* * *

The one magical aspect of recovery is having people who support and love me. I could not have ever landed safely and with such a strong force moving forward if it had not been for the people in my life. As I mentioned earlier, it is my relationships and connections with others that matter most to me, and now that I have recovered, I get to enjoy them.

For every person reading this who has been impacted by mental illness, I want to tell you how incredibly strong you are. Unless a person has lived with mental illness or with a loved one who has mental illness, it's hard to grasp how difficult the journey can be. The stress, the drama, the loss of time with loved ones—the list of pain and sorrow is endless. No one can ever comprehend what it takes to walk in the shoes of those of us who have lived a lifetime with the impact of mental illness, but people can have empathy and compassion with a greater understanding. This is another reason why it is important to talk openly about mental illness and to share our stories of struggle and triumph.

With great pain also comes the ability to feel great joy for the little things in life that make big differences. And there is always hope for a story shared to help another person's journey become a little easier. I never want to repeat any of the hard lessons I have learned, but my past has led me to my present, and for this I am humbly grateful. I know my calling is to continue being the best mental health advocate and speaker I can be and help as many people as God puts in my path.

I live my life by the words of Winston Churchill. "Never give up. Never give in. Never. Never. Never."

Chapter 26

Mental Health Advocacy Organizations

My family was facing mental health crises at the time when there was not easy access to information. One great thing about the Internet today is the ability to find everything you want to know about a mental illness. I know it would have helped me to understand what was happening.

This is why mental health advocacy organizations, such as NAMI (National Alliance on Mental Illness), are so incredibly beneficial. NAMI is the largest grassroots mental health advocacy organization in the United States. They work to help people who live with mental illness and their loved ones. NAMI also advocates for legislation that benefits the cause. It was founded by two sets of parents who had children with severe mental illness.

Parents who have children living with mental illness founded the NAMI of Greater Wheeling affiliate I have become involved with. They have been a beacon of hope for the community for more than thirty years. Today, they operate a drop-in or peer recovery center called the Marian House for adults who live with mental illness. It serves as a place where people can come after they have been stabilized and participate in numerous activities. My only wish is that every community could be as fortunate as ours and have a recovery center.

Another organization that does incredible work is Mental Health America. Mental Health America (MHA), founded in 1909, is the nation's leading community-based nonprofit dedicated to addressing the needs of those living with mental illness and to promoting the overall mental health of all Americans. They work to promote mental health as a critical part of overall well-being. Mental Health America advocates for early identification and treatment *before Stage Four*, which essentially means we need to treat mental illness before it gets to the most critical stages with the consequences of homelessness, joblessness, or incarceration.

The Depression Bipolar Support Alliance (DBSA) is a peer driven organization with support groups in every state around the country. They focus on providing tools and resources to empower people living with depression or bipolar disorder to achieve sustainable wellness.

The International Bipolar Foundation was founded by a mother whose son is impacted by bipolar disorder. They provide hope through their large social media presence and many online resources for people to learn more about bipolar disorder and how to manage it.

There are many more organizations who do tremendous work. If you are in need of support, education, or advocacy, I suggest you do a simple Google search of whatever mental illness you are looking for and include advocacy in your search. You don't have to walk the journey with mental illness alone. There are many people who are willing to help and support you, no matter if you are living with a mental illness or if you have a loved one affected by it.

I had it all, and I needed help, but I didn't know where to turn. I fought and survived, and now I'm thriving. You are strong enough to do it too. You are not alone, and there is no shame in having a mental illness. You got this!

One Final Poem

Hope Finds Me

If I could humbly see my way
Open up my eyes today
Lord please help me find-the open door

Darkness comes upon my soul
My faith is weary and at foe,
Send the angels one more time
To save me in the night

Sunset leaves a bright orange streak
Hanging in the painted clouds
In that picture perfect view
I find a little smile

My heart opens one more time
Ancient wisdom I seek to find
In the moment, hope, finds me

~Amy Gamble

What is Bipolar Disorder?

According to the National Institute of Mental Health, bipolar disorder, also known as manic-depressive illness, is a brain disorder that causes unusual shifts in mood, energy, activity levels, and the ability to carry out day-to-day tasks.

People having a manic episode may:
• Feel very "up," "high," or elated
• Have a lot of energy
• Have increased activity levels
• Feel "jumpy" or "wired"
• Have trouble sleeping
• Become more active than usual
• Talk really fast about a lot of different things
• Be agitated, irritable, or "touchy"
• Feel like their thoughts are going very fast
• Think they can do a lot of things at once
• Do risky things, like spend a lot of money or have reckless sex.

People having a depressive episode may:
• Feel very sad, down, empty, or hopeless
• Have very little energy
• Have decreased activity levels
• Have trouble sleeping, they may sleep too little or too much
• Feel like they can't enjoy anything
• Feel worried and empty
• Have trouble concentrating
• Forget things a lot
• Eat too much or too little
• Feel tired or "slowed down"
• Think about death or suicide

About the Author

Amy Gamble is a mental health author and speaker. She is also the Executive Director of NAMI Greater Wheeling, WV. She lives peacefully in Sherrard, West Virginia and is active in her community.

Made in the
USA
Lexington, KY

54328515R00139